ASSARACUS

A JOURNAL OF GAY POETRY
ISSUE 12

SIBLING RIVALRY PRESS
ALEXANDER, ARKANSAS
siblingrivalrypress.com

EDITOR & PUBLISHER

Bryan Borland

ASSOCIATE EDITOR

Seth Pennington

Cover photograph by Cody Henslee. Used by permission.

All rights reserved. No part of this book can be reproduced in any form by any means without written permission. Please address inquiries to the publisher:

Sibling Rivalry Press
13913 Magnolia Glen Drive
Alexander, AR 72002
info@siblingrivalrypress.com

Printed in the United States of America.

ISBN: 978-1-937420-58-1
ISSN: 2159-0478

Assaracus: Issue 12.
October 2013.

POETRY BY

DERRICK AUSTIN ... 7

DAVID BERGMAN ... 20

JOE ELDRIDGE ... 27

ROBERT HEALD ... 44

GARY LUNDY ... 57

JEFF OAKS ... 66

CHRISTOPHER PHELPS ... 78

STEVEN RIEL ... 90

JACKSON SABBAGH ... 102

ROBERT WHITEHEAD ... 116

EMANUEL XAVIER ... 125

STEPHEN ZERANCE ... 138

CONTRIBUTORS ... 147

DERRICK AUSTIN

Hounds of Memory

DON'T FEED THE WOLF

Strawberries, mangoes, first fruits of summer,
                and I can't afford to buy.
     They blush in bins, unashamedly sweet.

My wolfish face, unshaven, glides past joggers,
             women fanning themselves.
   A vendor waves me down: *Uvas?*

Grapes on sale. He sneaks three, winks,
           and pops them into his mouth,
  one at a time. Don't feed the wolf.

I'll bite. I'll steal. I'll lick your sweat
           until it blushes into wine. Don't
  feed the wolf. I'll wear you down

with how long I can wait.

PASS-A-GRILLE

I look for you on the storm-smoothed shore,
        glittering where the moon tows across
the bay. Cool air hangs its mints in my lungs

as I walk past sea oats, past sea grapes
        in tidal pools. Waves spread foam
like playing cards—a flush the land can't beat—

and the sea keeps upping the ante: first,
        quartz and crysolite, then breakwaters
and wooden weirs, then the land itself,

an erosion so ceaseless I too want to give
        my body, wholly, to something else.
Camped by a fire, you call to me.

The sea shuffles its indifferences, the way
        desire moves in us, wearing us down,
indifferent to who offers himself—

swimming, coasting, rowing, or floating
        face down. The lighthouse
winks its one good eye. The hull of a tank ship rusts.

Mouth to mouth, we're our own drowning.
        And if we're found,
your skin will be blue linen all over my body.

CHANSONS D'AMOUR

In the French musical of our lives
you are the Breton boy in orange briefs

smoking Gauloises and reading Proust
without irony. Leaning on the balcony's ledge,

I peer through your window—
Parisians swan down streets lit gold and blue

below my feet. I sing against detachment,
I sing you out; I sing your kiss,

the tricks of your postmodern tongue.
The April-cold rain rings like a strain by Satie.

We're lured by music. Music beats us.
Come inside, you say. *The cops are talking us down.*

CATACOMBS OF SAN CALLISTO

He's never Himself in the earliest frescos:
the shepherd boy guarding the sallow lamb
whose fleece might hide the god. Or the fish

and bowl of loaves. Or the phoenix.
He's isn't Himself, yet I trust Him.
I've walked alone with a man in the dark

and made much of his body—
you're with me now, touring the nests of the dead.
We're told by books old as these walls:

Filthy, our bodies, yours and mine. Not so.
When we love, we take each other in
like living water until we come, and warm

plaits of air unbraid in our throats.
The early artists did not turn up their noses
to flesh and, in this way, honored

the putrefying bodies in their midst,
painting the signs by which their bodies
would be watched and known.

The liquid issue smeared those newly-minted
frescos with scents of urine and blood.
I would gladly shame myself in this way for you.

I would be the good shepherd
above your body in its cold, stone niche
not only because I believe

in the resurrection of the body, but because
I want to be the face that welcomes you
to that inordinate dark.

THE LAST CASTRATO

If not the best, at least last
        to hold that longed for note

prized by priest and emperor,
        and to your modern ears, yes,
my voice creaks, but I was old

when I recorded this,
and who would doubt my grace
        notes in my prime?

I could polish air,
a hundred champagne glasses ringing,
ringed with golden fizz.

If only I could hold that note forever.

Pinned, pearled, and feathered,
grande dames of the continent praised me:
a tear in each note, a sigh in each breath.

I peacocked at concerts,
        silk scarf signing the air.

If not the best, then dress
the role. Call me your angel,
the smallest one who begs

no pardon because no one would hear.
        If not the best, then last—
hear it one more time, a sapling note
from the apple I never thought would grow,
        and in this man's body
a woman's voice, a delicate song
cutting the sweetmeat of my throat.

SELF-PORTRAIT AS GRETA GARBO
IN *QUEEN CHRISTINA*

Last night, disguised as a man, I revealed
my breasts to you, yet you did not

kiss them. They were not snowdrifts
but unbound, disorienting as the blizzard

locking us in this cabin. When you look at me
I see myself in you as king,

as bride always departing. I shall die a bachelor.
I would cut my hair and bring down

all twenty-four ribs, white pillars, on your heart.

RADIANCE

You're gone. Of course I'm burning our old photos,
my postmodern odalisque. We're wet in this one.
Remember shaking the water from that sycamore?
The fire dries our clothes and eyes, wrings the sky black.
There we are, not yet gone, old selves unblossoming.

I imagined our love as a fire that consumed darkness
and light. Your breath, in sleep, said *we are not ashes,
not ashes* as I leaned in to listen. My eyelashes try
beating the fire out, these tears a transmutation of fire,
these tears a departure, the same cry of your body in mine.

JEZEBEL

You sniffed me out like a prophet
after a problem and a city filled with people
who never listen. I nursed a longneck
by the cooler, catfish on ice jeweled
with flies. You were slick and coffin-sharp.
Haven't we had this date from the start?
You promised to make it snow in May,
which reminds me—too late—of Borges
on love and fallible gods. I believed
the world crystallized for you.
Snow collected on the crown of my head.
No. You flicked cigarette ashes on me.
Touch me, touch me. O hounds of memory!
All night gnawing and lapping my palms.

GOLD NIMBUS
FOR NARISA

Tumblers handy, you supply the Tanqueray
and scroll of lilac-scented hair I breathe
leaning on your shoulder (an old flame stung
memory's ungraceful hand). Your necklace's
gold Buddha shines. Once your grandmother's,
it was her gift to you after her funeral—
also there: chanting monks and offerings of fruit,
your father, his mistress, and a land dispute.
Anger, pain, and tears chained to that charm
and, quietly as breath, as soon let go.
Here I am, tipsy, the least Zen being
in the room. Even your gold nimbus of a dog
lapping your empty palm, content with salt,
lives with joy tucked behind his ears.

ARRIVAL AT KEY WEST

To get away from it all,
        I mill through crowds
antsy to get off the cruise ship,

the brochure promising rest and the sweetest
        chocolate key lime pie.

Instead chickens greet me;
chickens knifing each other with talons
        in alleys, on stoops.

They strut like Aunt Vera;
        in a photo
gold hoops on, she cracks a Heineken bottle
across her cheating husband's skull—
fifteen stitches later, their ten-year anniversary.

Ferocity, the only trait
        I didn't pick up from my women.

On Front Street, I get my picture taken
with cast-iron Hemingway. His skin stings mine.
(O Papa won't you waltz with me?)

Past banyans, a school tethered to vines,
        the lighthouse (worth the climb),
and an altar to Our Lady of the Keys
is the Southernmost Point's graffiti'd buoy.
        What a joke.

It gets a hell of a lot lower than this.

I think of you packing up and leaving
        in a rush for Rio or Australia, anywhere far,
wild, where everything's reversed
even the flush and shower drain.
I don't expect the heart to work the same.
        It was my fault. Bedroom aside,
there comes a point when begging just degrades.

Headphones on, I listen to "Queen of the Night,"
"The Sun Will Rise," and "Devil's Spade,"
        songs with names like the flowers

spiraling down waterspouts and door frames.
Tendrils and trunks reclaim a block,
        gutted houses overwhelmed
        by the kapok's buttressed roots.

Even the dirt road to the cemetery lifts
and dips like waves
                of a heart monitor.
The sun bleaches tombstones Clorox white.

Mausoleums above ground remind
even the dead are moved
by torrents bearing down.

Where you rest may not be where you stay.
Even we will cling for dear life,
emblazoned on an alabaster vault.

Moss frames a headstone, illegible
        except *Novenas por Jacinto*,
his body long ago conveyed to higher ground.
The grave's been worn by water and the oil
        of hands, the elements
that carried me here. Sleepless. Changed.

ODE ON A COWBOY'S ASS

As if from faded tintypes, wanted signs,
and film, symbol of the Wild West, proud man
without a cattle drive, and lacking all
intent to prove your worth, except with rake
and gardening gloves, God bless those Wranglers
pressed against your ass. Strutting to the shed,
your gait is clipped (friction's way of saying
strike a pose). You're the real deal: belt buckle,
farmer's tan sans T-shirt. I'd pay a grand—
a million to build the Lone Star State
a Louvre, to see you statuesque and nude.
Darling, let's get Aristotelian.
The space between denim seams divided
by our distance equals a golden mean.

But there's no time for symmetry and math.
You work fast. Etymology will do—
not "cowboy" but those globes of yours. That ass.
I've wasted too much time on wit, conceit.
Bless the sailor sick of rot and salt, blue-
balled on the docks, who caught an arse so snug
in whites he clipped the useless letter off.
Off they went to explore each other's worlds
until their stars were spent, at last exhaust
the possibilities of tongue. But seas
and language mean nothing to you, trimming
hedges under the wax-white summer sun,
shirtless but for threads of sweat and pale grass.
All men need new beginnings and here's yours:

You pound elements into submission,
no time for airs when earth must be molded
and made useful. Your ass plows vacant plots.
Your ass builds nations. Your ass is epic
in dirty jeans like James Dean's in *Giant*.
In the age of cant and kitsch, can beauty
be heroic? You bend to weed your lawn,
ripping crabgrass heads like ragged denim
as muscle fibers fray and mend, borders
of a nation, your body one country
I see myself moving in. My cowboy,
is this how men are made? Rolling in dirt?
Your end is where I begin. Pen in hand:
Sing, O muse, of the ass of Achilles.

David Bergman

Calm at the Periphery

DESTINY

Destiny is what we make
out of what we have:

a dog whose haunches are too big
for the ottoman on which he's sleeping,

a pile of books so high it's ready
to topple over, a black man

screaming in the street, a Saturday
in September cooler than expected.

Destiny is a poem, a poem we've written
when we could've written something else.

IMMORTALITY

How much nearer immortality was
for the ancients. To discuss it you might need

to send the flute boy out and free the room
of all distraction. But then you had the stars

to bring the infinite close to hand,
or the sunset, a glory to transcend

the gold-flecked air. The very stone of the floor
seemed freshly drawn from the primal earth,

and the breeze that fingered your beard was as cool
and relentless as if it had blown across

the void and howled its way between the darkness
and the light. Were not the trees goddesses

gone wrong? The tongueless birds warbling rape?
Under such condition how could death not

seem a doorway to the everlasting
one needed to knock just once for entrance?

For them the planet buzzed above their heads
in perfect harmony. Or was that wine?

No matter. Today we are forced to take
one day at a time and play the hopscotch

of ten-step plans, our immortal longings
left at the door like mud-encrusted shoes.

And the flute boy? He just left with the cook
for a wild weekend in Vegas.

FIRST MOAN

Children cry; the old moan.
Age teaches them by rote
how to form it in the gut
and extrude it through the throat.

They make it when they're dying
or when resisting death,
after they've stopped crying
and put fear out of reach.

They've used sex for practice
standing, squat or prone
at the height of their arousal,
with others or alone.

Hips are thrust far forward,
pace lowered or increased,
the sound sucked throbbing inward,
and bit-by-bit released.

SEPTEMBER SONG

Two days of steady rain have cleared
the streets of summer.

Sure, after awhile, it will stagger back
like a wayward boyfriend

with cockamamie stories of where he's been.
But it's over, you tell yourself, and pretend

relief. Even in the heyday of the romance,
you knew he wasn't the type to stick around.

Not with those rippling sinews of heat,
the granite butt, the lumbering stride,

as he paraded around naked.
Forget the promises he made. He was never

going to help around the house. Never.
It's time now to pull out the old wardrobe

and see if the pants still fit,
break open the binding of that book

you've been keeping on your night stand
and weep for the insipid heroine

taken in by Lord Manosex, when the bland
Reverend Autumn loved her all along.

DAVID BERGMAN

THE PROSPECTOR OF WORDS

The prospector of words stands in the flat
field behind his house, knee-deep in dry grass,
unshaded by the few scrub trees, withered
pine and cedar, while agitated birch
try to stay calm at the periphery.
In the distance, he sees hills and beyond
them mountains that he has yet to visit.

He has tried diving with every rod
that he could find—hickory, laurel,
oak and holly—but returned to willow
in the end because he feels in its spare
tenderness the faint powers that draw it
downward. He holds the rod lightly in hands
that may have grown too rough for such green limbs.

He opens and closes his eyes unsure
which would make him more alert to the twinge
of the hidden that is as subtle as
the liar's twitch when inadvertently
the liar tells the truth. To feel so weak
and brief a force, he must put everything
out of his mind: the unperturbed sun;
the sweat that swarms around his head and stings

his eyes; the boulders like squatters who fight
each attempt at eviction; the dark, ripe
stench of the dead—all must be forgotten.
He will remain motionless and empty
to let whatever stirs come from without,
reaching him only as it travels up
through what he's learned to carry with respect.

DREAMS I DO NOT REMEMBER

Most of my dream I throw back to the dark
like fish pulled from the bottom of a lake.

How they wriggle at the end of my line,
helpless and glittering in the weak dawn.

They are too small to pull into the boat.
They slip out of my hands when I grab them.

The big ones are as rowdy as barracuda.
They leave my arms aching in the morning

with the effort of bringing them on board
I would like to stuff these dreams and mount them

above the mantel. "This one took all night
to reel in," I'd boast and you'd have no choice

but to admire it: the great, knife-sharp
gills, the bristling fins, the mirthless blank eye.

DAVID BERGMAN

THE REMAINS OF PLEASURE

The summer is heavy with it.
Twilight bends low, hauling it

into the house. Gulls cry
exhausted by it, and the trees

rock in the crosscurrents
of its fatal beat.

Its thin film sticks
to my skin then spreads

like a slick in the warm bath.
At night I breathe it in,

and it slumbers
in the crook of my aching arm.

JOE ELDRIDGE

KISSING JIMI HENDRIX

FLIGHT HOME

Last leg of trip—it's right after takeoff
so I'm harnessed in my jumpseat
holding *USA Today* in my lap
daring to peak at the puzzle
when a portly woman, dead-ringer
for my decades-old fag hag (same
jungle red lips & nails) bolts down
the aisle to my exit door
sinks to her knees & it's the panic
in her eyes that I'm gripped by
when she tells me she's in recovery
Beefeater gin her booze of choice
five years since she'd bottomed out
in Paris of all places but so wanted
a sober return to the boulevard
where a gendarme found her drunk
face down in debris & dog droppings

& this visit having survived the bistros
sidewalk cafés, prix fixe dinners
with a bottle of burgundy
as the centerpiece, right now
a can of beer as blue collar as Coors
sings out to her as clearly
as Marilyn Monroe's married lover
Yves Montand, crooning "Come back to me"
so could I please honor
her unconventional request & page
for a friend of Bill W or anybody
to keep her from climbing inside
a liquor cart, the countless cups of coffee
to talk her through the next eight hours
trapped in this tin flask.
I say—*My name is Joe. Speak to me.*

MOTHER LOVED TO JOKE

       on her knees
the preacher's wife

pulling straight pins
from her lips

hemming
sister's Sunday frock

draped on Twiggy me
the dress dummy

& as if quoting scripture
she'd quip:

all the world old is queer
save me & thee

& even thou art
a little queer

then laugh
full-on belly grab

until her dentures
begged for realignment—

but stopped laughing
when I kissed a boy

in fact—hasn't chuckled
at that chestnut since.

DAD WHITTLED A WALKING STICK

        out of a four foot oak branch
as big as Merlin's staff—
the memory of it
all knotty & knife-marked.

He prepared Old Testament
sermons in the solitude
of cornfields
communing with God

in King James's eloquent tongue
but at the supper table
he'd point & grunt
for a drumstick & biscuit

& if response to his hunger
wasn't quick enough
his cracked leather belt
voiced his displeasure.

Recently, I asked my siblings
about the dusty stick
propped against his La-Z-Boy—
if it was the same

he favored to ward off snakes
when he strolled the gravel
paved roads after he preached
hellfire on Sundays.

Brother said, "Chase me
though the house
& whack me on the back
with it, then I'll be able to tell."

STEVE MCQUEEN

Captain on a flight I worked
dropped his kitbag at the cockpit door
told me I look like Steve McQueen.

Senior flight attendant in the forward galley
preflight said, "Hey, you know who
you look like? Steve McQueen."

Passenger in the twilight zone of coach
buying a carton of Marlboro Red from duty free
said, "You look just like Steve McQueen."

I asked each if they thought I looked like him
before or after he developed asbestos-related cancer
then dashed to the handicap lav with the full length mirror.

"He was the king of cool," the first officer quipped.
"Hot man on a motorcycle," a coworker cracked.
"Loved you in *Bullitt*," 12J joked.

I stood a little taller, wondered the relevance
of resembling an actor dead for three decades.
Could I get work as a celebrity look-alike?

U.S. customs official opened my passport
held it to my face and asked
if anyone ever told me I look like Steve McQueen.

I exited the international terminal with a new pep
in my step, jumped on the tram
bloated with Hollywood headiness.

JOE ELDRIDGE

My Match.com coffee date at Caribou chided,
"You would've been easier to spot if you'd told me
how much you look like Steve McQueen."

Mental note: pick up retro jeans and T-shirts
perhaps a few *Thomas Crown Affair* ensembles
keep hair clipped, practice acting like an icon.

BIG SISTER HAD A MEXICAN BOYFRIEND

When I look at dark-skinned men, I cannot help
but return to 1969—Daddy's just sermonized
at his very own Freewill Baptist—the text:
"Sonny & Cher—Communists!" Next door
in the parsonage kitchen, I'm singing—*Bang,
bang my baby shot me down*—while pleating
paper towels into beautiful Japanese fans
setting out jelly glasses for supper
hoping the Kool-Aid's grape.
In the living room, Mother tightens
her bun with hairpins & tucks her skirt
behind her calves. Dad, still full
of that old-time religion, paces
the rug & adjusts his patriotic necktie
while humming "Just As I am," the last altar-call
song he'd requested before concluding
the morning church service. Big Sister
her Breck-girl hair ironed straight
down her beauty pageant back
with just the correct tone of deference
introduces her boyfriend, who an hour earlier
in his Grand Prix, slipped an opal
on her promise finger & when Dad
scrutinizing the beau's coloration
asks where his people come from
Sister quickly chirps—*He's Mexican*.
Then I hear a bubbly baritone
sing out—*Chili today and hot tamale*
accompanied by cackling laughter & backslapping
Dad, of course, sharing his best Tijuana weather joke
then not another word in that part of the house—silence.

JOE ELDRIDGE

As I check the Shake N Bake chicken for burns
Dad comes into the kitchen, leans on the countertop
looks me squarely in the eyes & says none too softly—*Son
that's a nigger out there. Don't ever bring one of those home*
then returns to Sister's guest to recount, I'm fairly certain
some rib-tickler about watermelons.

That night I dreamed of kissing Marvin Gaye
no—better than that—kissing Jimi Hendrix
no—better yet—kissing the Tuesday morning trash man
his biceps as black as the onyx on Dad's pocketknife
& his lips—his thick glistening lips pressing into mine.

JOE ELDRIDGE

BIG BROTHER HAS A LITTLE FARM

Pony foundered
died before he could be put down
carted off in a pickup's bed to be buried
as promised by the vet

The pygmy goat, now the favorite pet, floats
Chagall-like to the shed roof
comes down to eat cigarettes & leafy branches
his old man Vandyke circling like a hula dancer

Feeding him has become your only pleasure
you once said, leisure time eaten up mowing the massive lawn
can't get local boys to do it
they're all in 4H with hayfields to bale & bulls to geld

There's no time for iced tea in the gazebo
skinny-dipping in the heated pool
the asparagus patch has gone the way of the rabbits
barn cats lost to possums & foxes

That's just farm life, you say
not a minute to visit
bake a lemon chess pie
barely time to reheat Pizza Hut

So we don't speak anymore as we often did
thought we would at the last family shindig
but you none too subtly sidestepped me
to refill your rocks glass

In a quieter moment
when pressed about the silent treatment

JOE ELDRIDGE

you stage-whispered, "You know full well why"
turned your back, lit a Marlboro Red

& I suppose I could tell you again
"Sorry I blew your husband"
but thought that was all covered when I sobered up
ninth-stepped you—apparently not.

PANCREATITIS

I've never been t-boned
by a dune buggy on Fire Island
or garroted by a hand painted
silk scarf in Nice

Never choked on a bottle cap
in the Elysee Hotel
or been found face down
in a bubble bath in the Beverly Hilton

I've never swallowed a toothpick
which perforated my bowel
causing fatal peritonitis
on a luxury liner to Brazil

No autoerotic asphyxiation for me
in Bangkok or Sea Bay
No Valentino's dildo
gagging me in Brentwood

Contrary to popular belief, I did not doll
myself up in my Hollywood hacienda
down eighty Seconal tablets
eat a burrito *con frijoles y arroz*

retire to my perfumed bedchamber
to await sweet *muerte*
but, *ay Dios mio*, a mariachi band struck up
"*Sabor a mi*" in my belly and on my way

to the powder room to puke
tripped in my come-fuck-me pumps

JOE ELDRIDGE

conked my head on the porcelain rim
and drowned in pee water

No, none of those necrologies
happened to me
at the Walter Payton Liver Center
I merely nearly died of something stupid.

JOE ELDRIDGE

MAKING IT IN THE MEATPACKING DISTRICT

1984, standing room only for
La Cage Aux Folles, I braced
myself against the rail to mouth
along with "the best of times is
now," marveled after the musical
when I bumped into a gypsy
outside the Palace, gushed that
he was an amazing dancer
told him I nearly died when he
pulled off his girl-wig at the end
of "I Am What I Am" to reveal
the beautiful boy he actually is.
I sensed he was off to cruise
the Village as I followed him
past 42nd Street, didn't realize
he was a member of the S&M
demimonde until there we were
in the Mine Shaft—a collage
of burning cigars, black leather
harnesses, Muir caps, ass-less
chaps, nipple rings, piss-stained
jockstraps. I'd been to tea dance
at the Gold Coast in Chicago
on more than one Sunday
was popular in the basement
though I avoided the trough, but
here in Manhattan I quickly came
to the realization that I was
far too pretty for this fist
fucking crowd. They blew me
off like I was the common clone.
No luck at the Spike or the Eagle

either. The Anvil where the metallic
gym short wearing Studio 54 men
liked to slum it was more welcoming.
A drag queen swaddled in a ripped
white satin sheet held together
with diaper pins lip-synced to
"Bette Davis Eyes" while teetering
on the bar in battered pumps.
The archetype of a macho man
in all his Adam-in-the-garden glory
swayed in a sling suspended
from the ceiling with chains.
He pulled his knees straight up
to his hirsute chest, shucked
the lid off a can of Crisco
& proffered it to the frenzied
group of shirtless men dancing
around him passing poppers
from nose to nose. I like to think
the mature Marlboro man
in the Brooks Brothers suit
who I shotgunned a joint & made
out with, our tongues probing
like pickaxes digging for diamonds,
was the American art collector
& curator, Sam Wagstaff
& the much younger than he
bare-chested pretty guy
who looked like he just woke up
at the Chelsea Hotel when he
joined us in the Drakkar Noir
dark, feathered his fingers
through my hair then skinned
his hand inside my Calvin Klein's
pressed his spit-moist thumb

to my silky bulls-eye as he trapped
my jugular vein with his Jagger lips
was the hot daddy's lover, famed
photographer Robert Mapplethorpe.
Who's to say they weren't?

JOE ELDRIDGE

DIAMOND HEAD IN ONE ACT

My autobiographical play's plot is unique only to me.
Exposition begins with the sun flittering
like a prismatic koi in a reflecting pool.
We ascend the crater's interior on the concrete
walkway lifting our legs like Lipizzaner stallions.
We're well into the rising action as we maneuver
the switchback that traverses ankle-twisting slopes
through wild grasses and Koa trees housing doves
that really do coo. He emotes eureka recognition
pointing out that the cardinals in Kiawe bushes
are like those perched on electrical lines back home.
We continue the ascent on manmade stairs as steep
as those I've seen in pictures of Machu Pichu
and as terrifying too. Now this is the point
in the plot where we wait, he and I, hanging
onto iron rails until his laborious breathing
and arrhythmic heartbeat settle into something
like stasis. This is when I mouth a soliloquy
praying he'll achieve a tranquil equilibrium
and make it to the top for his mother, my sister,
would never forgive me if his heart gave out here.
His pulse lessens so we step into the lightless tunnel
the air as cool as a root cellar's in late summer
and for the final section, we belly crawl
through the gap that admits us to the summit.
Our senses astound to the scent of hibiscus
and jasmine as we look down onto Waikiki Beach
where morning surfers glide in Tai Chi meditation.
To the left, at Koko Head, humpback whales
breach, geysers erupting from their blowholes.

This is the climax. This is where I desperately
want the story to end, the shared moment
when he and I grasp onto a full measure of time
to exalt in just being in uncontained bliss.
The rest is falling action and God I do not want
the denouement as written. Seven years pass
like Auntie Mame at the banquet. He's home
in the Gayborhood stretched out on his recliner
favorite blanket pulled up to his chin,
a sundrenched smile on his face. "He looked
peaceful," the local sheriff said after
performing a wellness check and finding him.

ROBERT HEALD

Carolina Solitaire

BODY UNKNOWN

You see him leaning against the wall by the cardboard
pillars of Oz at the high school prom   hovering
at the outer rim of conversation   You remember
the sidelong glance when you stepped on his toes
on the dance floor earlier   but now his date is nowhere
to be seen   You are struck by the pure ease
the nonchalance of his silence   so like your own
but more sure   Your eyes trace the line of his jaw
to where it meets the neck in that cleft below the ear
You keep going   faint blonde stubble   lips loosely closed
the aquiline nose   until with a cold shock
you realize he's seen you   You flee
pretending to be hungry   thirsty   anything
embarrassed and ashamed at your own stirring heart

Midnight finds you at the afterparty
standing in a corner   not really wanting to talk
to anyone   You stare into the bottom

of your empty cup   No   I can't be   I don't want
this   None of the songs will be true anymore
All I wanted was Mary's dress   the slamming screen door
Springsteen's girl who ain't a beauty   but hey she's alright

A throat clears   jolts you out of yourself
and he's there in front of you   as if he had been
all along   Somewhere a tower crumbles
a levee breaks   and you feel even before he speaks
that something has gone and is never coming back

You know what will follow   The fumbling touches
the brush of fingertips across the back of a hand
a leg just barely pressing another   a look
a whisper   *I don't know if I   It's alright
I don't   I can't   I'm afraid   Did you think
it would be easy*   And all at once you let yourself go
allowing the rush of blood to take over   to course
through you   to drive you   to lead your lips
to his

Five in the blue spring morning   it wasn't how you thought
you'd feel   watching the rise and fall
of his chest   almost too much   almost
not enough   You ask yourself   *What have I done
Who have I become*   But his eyes open   and God
with his fruit knife   slices off the best piece of the apple
of your being   to eat for his breakfast

Something falls away   leaving you clean and hollow
like the day you got your driver's license and drove alone
to the grocery store   how you wandered
up and down the aisles   just being apart   tasting a new existence
But not without a kind of sadness   do you rise
that morning   to a world somehow smaller   with one less
mystery to discover   one less silence to break
one less body unknown

CAROLINA SOLITAIRE

The Atlantic goes on breaking itself
against the Carolina shore   while you walk out
to where he stands   the surf around his ankles
facing the sunrise   You are seventeen
There's a girl still sleeping in the house at your back
and together they are pulling you apart
while you know the seams cannot hold
You agreed to go for a run this morning
Not your idea   but you'll do all you can
for that half hour alone with him
When you reach him   place your hand
lightly on the shoulder blade   he smiles
and your soul rises with your breath
out of your body   suspended in the salt air
for all of a single heartbeat   before he takes off
ahead of you as always

Later in the iron spring day   you'll sit
on the porch   playing solitaire
jack of hearts   queen of diamonds
the cards spinning out your story
But now heart's king has changed
his suit   *I like the way these diamonds sparkle*
And so you must face the dragons alone

How it begins you'll never remember
snap of the hangman's rope   the floor
dropping out   shadows dancing
on the wall   And then the hangman
takes off his hood to show you the haunted face
in the mirror   But however it begins
your eyes are on fire   and amid the noise

of blood in your ears   you notice
as not before how tightly your fists can clench

It's a long drive home from Carolina   a long time
to let the silence crackle between you
but as soon as he speaks your will breaks
and you give him all he wanted from you
nothing close to what you hoped   or imagined

In the Georgia hills once more   after dropping him off
and driving away   you sit in the corner diner
You've always liked the bitter comfort of the coffee
the smooth ceramic at your lips   the solitude
of the counter stool   But now
you eye the booths longingly
with their tables set for two   the mirrored
placemats and silverware an offering
to some god you've never known
Is there anything else you want   the waitress asks
Only what everyone wants   the girl
the boy   a corner booth   a second menu
Just another coffee please

THE RAINMAKER

I dare you   Her eyes shine darkly
in the flickering lights of passing cars   Do you really
think she won't   It's just the two of you
alone in your father's old Mustang   and the rain
is coming down on this highway to a promised land
called Clayton Georgia   Now you remember how she looked
all in white   hand so carefully entangled with your best friend's
at the high school dance   You recall the feeling of burning alive
and drowning at the same time   With every touch
every look passed between them   you were a child again
lost in the crowds of the amusement park   and the hands
all around you were not your mother's hands   and the voice
calling to you was not your father's voice

                                                      But you are here now
in your father's car   one hand sweating on the gearshift
the other white-knuckling the wheel   while she
is taking off her blouse   This is the game   you told her
one person sees a car with only one headlight   pounds the roof
and shouts pa-diddle   and the other loses a shoe
a shirt   a pair of jeans   It's only a game   not betrayal
not the breaking of boundaries you never knew you could break
looking wild-eyed into the jungles of a new world   A harmless game
until it's not   until you can't stop yourselves   until you both
are nearly naked   pale bodies luminous   seen only by a solitary trucker

It's not the softness of your body that nags you
but a half-heard voice crying in the back of your mind   the language
foreign and unintelligible   Years later you will realize
that you loved her   or thought you did   only because she was his
and that you loved him because he was everything

you both wanted   And that night   hurtling north on I-41
into the storm   you made the sorrow yourself
just like you made the rain

CONVERSATION AT TAQUERIA DEL SOL

On the outside terrace   at table number five
distracted by the taco shop's daily chaos
you clear your throat   trying to clear your mind
Just as the food arrives steaming   you speak to the horizon
above your parent's heads   and all at once there's no turning back
You are outside yourself   watching as the words
fall from your tongue   The tacos forgotten
the queso getting cold   the ice melting in your unsweet tea
while the world suspends in the air between you
and your father   Any moment it could fall and shatter
like your mother's favorite ceramic plate   olive green
when it slipped from your hands   and how on your knees
as you began collecting the shards   the mumbled apologies sounded weak
even to you   The words are bricks in your mouth
and when you speak them   you aren't even sure what you said
Your father only raises his eyebrows   waits for half of eternity
Are you sure   You are astonished   the question
so far beyond any scenario you imagined   not denial
not anger   not disappointment   not even
a slowly rising sea between your father's continent
and your own   So you laugh   unsure
of what response to make   And your father
mustering all the love he can in his own quiet way
only shrugs   *Ok then*   *Taco?*

HEARTACHE

Looking for your beginnings in the magnolia wood
Henry walks the road just beyond your sight   You follow him
because something tells you he knows the reason
home has never seemed so strange   Higher up
further in   the light falling through the trees   Henry
walks on   still lingering at the vanishing point
and you watch him disappear into the gloaming woods

When you rise from the tangle and ivy of your dreams
Henry is waiting at the corner   admiring
the dogwood blossoms   The snow has stopped falling
but it doesn't snow in Georgia   Home is so strange lately
The days waits in your hands   and breaks apart
when morning comes across the water   Henry
begins to walk   his hair spun with sunlight
You've never seen the streets so still   breathless
with a waiting   You wonder at the emptiness inside you
another question for Henry to answer   but he won't
He'll just walk to the silent end of dawn   *Tell me
Henry   please tell me where this road goes*
To skin and bone   to earth and rain
to glory and heartache

HERITAGE

Listen: demons run wild through my veins.
I was born to the dark brother, the Cain

of a nation. Behind my own, hard eyes
looked out across the slave fields
of Georgia's cotton kingdom, the sweet by-
and-by drifting from the mansion as the sun wheeled

in an iron blue sky. I was born
to a line of men doomed to seek
the beautiful reward from which there is no return.
Bones and drunkards' vomit dammed the creeks,

and the crops of this land still taste of blood.
One morning I woke to find whatever goodness
still crouched in the corner of my heart dragged through mud,
beaten, tarred, and hung from the boughs of a cypress.

I am not the first, nor will I be the last,
only the inheritor of a nightmare legacy: whiskey,
bloody back, gray coat, a long passing
into ruin—so look away, look away, Dixie.

MORNING LIGHT

So let this be my wish for you, he says
in your dream. *Bravery and joy, all that's left
to hold back the darkness.* Waking, you watch him
rise from the bed, as dawn light seeps between
the cracks in your heart, a shattering when he runs
his fingers through his hair. Here, you could die,
only to become the daybreak falling through the glass,
the shadows rippling on his back.

THRESHOLD

Last night I dreamed of the house
my grandfather built   rising from water
in a sun torn morning   I watched the wind
run barefoot through the moonshiner's woods
murmuring to September's last sky   Where does
the story begin   and how does it end
This the story of our summers   the story
of our risings
                    Deep in the green beating heart
of the South   my father taught us to be kind
told us to be wise   And mama leave the light on
so I can find the way home   to your brown eyes
raising at the sound of an opening door   Here
my brothers were giants   my sisters were queens
of the morning
                    A bright May came
and all of a sudden we were older   more broken inside
and none of the pieces belonged anymore
So I drove into the horizon   climbed the sixteen stairs
to heaven   and poured those pieces into the sky

They say what is dead is never gone   and what is gone
is only forgotten   And last night   a raindrop
blew through the window   into my sleeping ear
And so the house   and the water   and the lights
of home   And so the screen door
swinging in the wind   And so the cradled jar of fireflies
burning over the threshold

THE PLACES YOU MADE

Here you are again, alone
with your aching eyes, your dry
mouth, your shaking hands. Here
are the ashes where you left them,
the stains on the counter, a darker stain
beneath your ribs you cannot scrub out.
Did you love them, Henry asks you
with his drowning eyes. *Did you love
him?* You had a dream where words
were spoken, and the words were beautiful
and so they were true, but every morning
you die all over again, opening your eyes
to an empty sky. Then sadness, yours
a mockingbird, flies to your window,
and stays the whole red day long.
Somewhere between shaving and showering,
you realize you've been here before:
the noon sun through the shutters, the snow
on the mountain, the vacant rooms,
the hunted heart in the mirror.

Here you are, with all your road
tangled behind your eyes, stars falling
into daylight. You begged Henry
to kiss you on the bridge while dawn
ripped the sky apart, but you open your fist
to let the day go, and Henry is gone,
sweat evaporating from your palm.
Your dry lips gasp for river water.
All you wanted was a voice, a sky to call
your own. All you wanted was a prayer,
to light yourself on fire and walk out into the rain.

ROBERT HEALD

Here is the place you made—the bed,
the books, the visions of flesh and light.
You speak your promise to the dusk falling
through the western window, but will you break
it in the morning, Henry standing in the door?
Look at the light shattering the silence, and hold
this hand of air and water. Kiss these fingers
of dust and light and tell me, try to tell me.

GARY LUNDY

Thousands of Miles

TODAY I CANNOT WORRY

about whether that *i* repositions the self as writing. rather. i look fondly toward the older man. my age. sitting across the room. red plaid shirt. long sleeve. blue t underneath. as he holds his glasses. you. bows toward the newsprint. i want to hold him. press a dear softly between us. touch the delicate skin of his shaved head. want him to meet my eyes in wanting this precise friday afternoon. to have him take me. to be taken. to his anonymous motel room. want him. wanting. to press his. such desire against me. to tear at my clothes. to fall onto my falling body hard. he poses gentle in longing across from me. and i want to believe. need to believe. that were he to ask to read this. were he to read this. his face would break into kindness. would touch my shoulder. would want to push me down onto my knees. down onto his bed. down onto the pressed pillow of his desire. would say. *i need to have you right now.* would take me. would fuck me. that we both might in such edifying lean across the space that separates. and the fear.

I GROW IMPATIENT WITH MY BODY

its manliness. this is not about castration. but about gentleness. i look in the mirror and see my fathers anger staring back. his hairy chest and arms. clean shaved face. short yellow-gray hair. how to retrieve my body from this weighted image. how to claim the delicacy of skin and pleasure. one wonders at the work ahead.

when i shower i feel sandpaper delusions. must sculpt and burn what i am into what my body tells me i must be.

i love you thoroughly. observe how you move between the lives of poetry fluid and powerful. *look me in the eyes.* blue against hazel. brown against green. take it down into hesitant memory.

when my body free of hair glistens in after shower moisture i return and see my lover. my mother. *you.* permit my hands and fingers to idle variously along the curves and palpability.

yet i remain absent. neither smooth skinned nor angry. neither mother nor father. neither your lover nor his.

i wash my body and feel your pleasures as i dwell bottomless. grow weary of my body. wonder where i might again find you.

IT IS NEVER ENOUGH TO WAIT

he knows that he has spent his life in waiting. for a moment to intrude so loudly into his solitude that he will have to move. to make a change. get to an altitude of being so lost he cannot help but follow. hoping not to perish.

when she visits such a moment brushes the left side of his face. a smile breaks out on both their faces. clarity suddenly revealed. a chain detaches from his voice and he talks and laughs himself into delirium.

no one notices. she is gone. left in mid-sentence. as he moved on and on out into the night of his disillusion. he looks up and notices. waits an answer. some vocal affirmation. a sign. which always fails to come.

alone again his eyes fill. dreams recount what might have happened. he could not know.

she drives past an insignificant mile marker. squints to keep disappointment at bay. forestall a rising fear.

they both hide. hope to hold to a moment that already has fled beyond memory.

he imagines there remains so much yet to say. but there isn't. really only long intervals of silence. its shapes and forms.

I WOKE THIS MORNING AN IMPOSSIBLE FLANGE OF MUSCLE ACHE

and memory loss. radical dream characters carried me through the hours. face upon face upon face until the faces blurred. all that remained. a set of eyes.

my lovers eyes. but you don't know him. she spins and twirls on tiptoes reaching out. down into the pureed bodies. liquifying desires drive to elope.

muscle memories until i can finally lift my head slightly off the pillow. push covers away. stand bound to gravity. a loss configuration.

you slept here. she did. your heads impression remains audible. my right ear tunes to the precise frequency. memory floods the floorboard of my first car. never exists in real time.

SO MANY REMAIN HIDDEN

remain discomforted by outside agitation. which represents internal turmoil. two pastors speak self-evasively. baptismal coffee break. their toes sweat inside their comfort shoes. their feet smell like my spit. your tears smell like the palm of my right hand. which smells like my spit. beneath the cotton fabric of my shirt my nipples harden. are you about to call me. or can it be the thrill of eavesdropping. crumbs of fear collect in their shoes. make walking a holy sacrifice. suffering. i must admit. i'm not in love with you. i don't even know what love is. an abstract idea. a chemical reaction under the skin. two men comfort each others right hands. prayer a stranger idea than love. which is a companion of despair. i cannot understand how her ass got so huge. an idea as image of her childhood. remember this has little to do with any of you. when i put the burgundy shoes on and look in the mirror i see my mothers legs. except once. and except with tattoos. i may be turning into an old woman. one who forgets to trim her toenails. popularity costs so much more than heat and utilities.

A SHOT. WHATEVER POSSIBILITY IT MIGHT AWAKEN TO.

forget burroughs. when i close my eyes. my lovers long fingers undress. i willow in mirror mistakes. an image. upon an image. upon another. last. image. you stop by briefly. and some new impossibility finds its way. through my locked door. what can it mean. to mean. to wear a womans skirt when the lights go off. you loved me. in those eyes that stretch out farther than reach. sublime wish wandering. he comes to my bed when i close my eyes. takes his pleasure. which is my pleasure. out on me. synchronous please.

I HAVE KILLED MYSELF

by not going down on the first man i fell in love with
he loved me the first time as forever
when he would take me i was the most beautiful girl on the block

i have killed myself for fondling
too many vaginas in a predictable failing attempt
to find love there

i have killed myself by moving away
from the second man i fell in love with twice
who would enter my apartment late at night
while my son slept and his wife dreamed of happiness
and while i did go down on him
and let him take me have me
i moved thousands of miles away in pretense twice

i have killed myself by staying here too long
and now being afraid of leaving

i have killed myself by believing this present one
underscored passion and unbridled taking
when all he could do was decipher everything into past tense

i have killed myself by permitting him to call me his boyfriend
simply because we are all we have here

i have killed myself believing the feeling i have had for you
and you is more than chemical biological

HE'S ONE. AND I WONDER. ONE WHAT.

she deliberately veils desires fear as one night stands. the wind carries rain. promise of cooler temps. so quiet now it is as if deaths white beard has put everyone asleep. a gift outside turquoise. time straddles sideways. paper quietly lifts then settles. a woman sings in a background free of obstacle. *to love*. a man carries me toward some metaphysical yes. as *yes*. with a language all his own. don't believe it for even a minute. a motorcycle charges through. breaks open this silence. fingers know no language. except skin. your skin sinks into a fast shiver. she smiles. looks up. as if. expecting more. lips part in whispered silhouette of yes. as *yes*. tonight. please. she marvels before his fear. his lack of courage. his frailty even. a vast masculinity.

IT'S NOT WHAT YOU THINK

i must learn how to separate idea from thing. but the idea looms large on my computer screen. your nude bodies. i love you moves out into the abstract. a wanting to touch as the idea. yet to avoid this. burrow down to the level of skin. when i think about you it's not with my dick in my hand. last night my dick smelled just like my spit. i don't feel like objectifying you any more. the idea is so much smaller. and the photos grainy when enlarged enough. maybe it's not about ideas or things. maybe it's all about the isolate self. as if that could be real either. displace idea with idea. my sweat smells just like my breath. my armpits are no longer smooth. a rash of hair brushes my tongue. a long tickle. when i piss i smell coffee. weird resemblance. so. when i think about you i need to forget it's not you. i need to forget about the thing in the idea that you could possibly. release the thing into my neighbors garden. rodent in japanese hip-hop. hope you don't remain offended. fixed. know escape. there's nothing about love here. maybe love is another idea outside any thing. not even a group. rock out to self-immolation. serious simultaneity.

JEFF OAKS

Ruthless Beauty

PARSNIPS

When did I start chewing the roots of things?
Roasted with salt and pepper. The pale kings
under the mountains. The young boy I once was
naked in the moonlight while my best friend
asked me questions about sex. Neither one of us
had a clue. Both of us thin and white
as these bodies whose skin I flay, whose
thick trunks I whittle down into slivers,
cubes. When he moved close one night,
I didn't refuse what he wanted to do.
It's a wonder I kept breathing. I was so afraid
the heat he made rise was blood I said
stop, that's enough. Later, at home, I did it though,
went all the way through the fear to another side
of myself. Stood after and looked in the mirror.
Thought I was beautiful to have survived.

LITTLE POEM AT 4 AM

That the dog the night before ate shit
until I called and called him and finally
stormed over to where he was, bent, face-down
in the grass; that he looked up nervously at last,

licking his chops like a kid taking one last hit
off a cigarette there was no hiding anymore;
that I took him to the river where I knew
he'd drink and drink away the awful smell

of what might have been human since all
the other dogs were showing such interest
(and there was a cast-off shirt nearby as well);
I remember this only after I've already been

kissing his dark head when he brings it near,
hearing me wake at 4 am. I can still smell in his fur
the river of terrible knowledge others, the ones
who lay down with betrayers, even murderers,

with the dying, sometimes must
keep kissing and kissing in spite of.
And be grateful for. Or: I try.
And hope even the trying is love.

THE END

After the definitions of mercy
are murdered, after the forks
removed, after the furniture
has been turned to face the future.
After the last toad has been
silenced, after the imaginable
violence of this machine or the next,
after the robot on the help line
admits it cannot help, please
try again later when another
robot will be working, after
the sickness has begun burning
your photographs, after the old
translations were finally revealed
to contain an unpronounceable stretch
of water neither flood nor river
nor trickle nor drought. After
the drought and its angry Protestants,
its brittle owls afraid to call out,
the quick mice and grass long since fallen
into a fine quiet rust. After the rain
reappeared and started shouting
from the porch about the lack
of love, the new Moon, the lost Stars.
After the last joke about the last
two priests going into the last straight bar
only to find the last lawyer there
already drunk and with the last
altar boy under his arm. After an armadillo
enters, says the punch line and explodes.
After the hush. After the last mask is ash.
Even after that. We will never get there.

POEM FOR THE SOLES OF MY FEET

who are constantly in the dark, are
constantly turned away from lights, are
wrapped in cloth and tied down, are
blindfolded like loaves of bread, like fresh fish,
like hostages and walked all day into
dead ends, through loud traffic, through
crowds, silences, water, gravel, hallways
full of hot cardomom, fennel, secret
cigarettes, muffled laughter, until they
are too tired to remember how to get back,
where to return, until they come to believe
they need us to survive, us to make meaning
out of their lives, opening and closing against the ground
like hearts open and close, sending blood back
up the columns of the legs again, bringing
blood down upon themselves, thirsty and sweating
into their masks, stuffed into tiny cars, faces
pressed into the heat of engines, the punch
of brakes, the slamming of doors, the pop
and shriek of locks, sudden pirouettes of
happiness, how they shuffle beneath us, growing
quietly, steadily desperate for the inexplicable
tickles and kisses of love, the slipping free
of covers to find another pair like themselves,
blazing like coals in the three AM darkness
and silence, and touching them with a tenderness
that surprises even themselves, that they still
have it in them, after all this time, like the fish
that wakes up in the pan and in its last second
forgives its devourer everything that will come next.

JEFF OAKS

SONNET DURING THE WARS

That language is what we know we must somehow
(we who use it to intensify the world into
its pieces or out of its fragmentariness) use:
a man walks by and his black sweater a moment

turns the window I look out of into a mirror
in which my face appears. In the news, various peace
projects seem to be moving along as do war
plans in other parts of the country, not here

where I am surprised at the way my face
has aged since the last war the country threw
itself into, since the last time the priests
turned the poor into recruits, the last time we had

as movie previews commercials for a military
whose motto's to rid the world of fairies.

AFTER GRIEF

There's an end to waiting but not right yet.
Let me sit here in the quiet a little bit more,
waiting for something other than breath
to move inside me, other than hunger,

other than thirst. There will be an end
but first I need to just wait. Eventually I will
get up from here and begin, get dressed,
make breakfast, take the dog out, get to work.

It won't take long but for now I need to wait
quietly like a tourist listening for new sounds
outside the window, inside my own mind,

finding myself in a strange bed and slowly
reciting to myself the few words I know
in the strange language I will have to use.

THE VIOLETS

Strangeness on simmer
in the corner
by the brickpile,

the violets
grow without an ounce
of self-pity,

a quiet flame
you can eat
if you're hungry,

in the shadow of the grill,
behind the snowshovel's
broken haft, the broom left

out to rot, flame in the crack
by the rake, in the lee
of the garbage cans,

a ruthless beauty—like
the ash of a burning school—eating
whatever dirt falls down.

OIL CHANGE

In the waiting room of the Jiffy Lube men
in blue helmets are playing others in white
on a loud TV just above the free coffee stand.
The manager says it's a shame about Pitt losing
last night by one point, isn't it, because it's just
the two of us in here and I'm staring at the screen
like someone who's interested. I say yeah, so
I don't burst his version of me, which is
that I'm like him in some way, because he seems
like a nice guy, smiling, unafraid of crawling
under cars, unscrewing things, replacing filters,
laughing with the other guys. Partly I want
whatever deal might come from this disguise.
Partly because I know that's not what it is:
either he's lonely and making small talk, or
he thinks I might be too and is trying to help.
That I was thinking about Frost's notion of
The Sound of Sense and the way football for me
falls into that category (I can tell something's there
from the rhythms and energy in the announcers' voices
even if the specific words have no meaning)
makes little difference. The white helmets
which he thinks is the better team are winning.

HURRICANE

Because we are warlike, we are superstitious.
Because we are superstitious, we seize upon meanings
whenever the wind changes, whenever rain
begins to fall. Whatever eases the pain
of strength without purpose, consciousness
without answer, a world of endless mirrorings
the rain makes worse, filling up the streets.

ORIOLE

I've only seen it as flashes
across the trail behind the fence
where the engineers at the Robotics Institute
test their driverless vehicles:
mowers guided by remote control,
the camouflage-colored truck rumbling
down the service road along the tracks,
guided by clean cut young men looking
into their hands. Where that orange
and black burst of flame has gone to,
I can't follow. It's a bird
with a name the tongue twists itself
to get right, to make it appear, bright
herald, half-blaze, half-shadow,
summer's wild cindered song.
Somewhere nearby is a nest
woven of grass and plastic, a brown scrotal
basket hanging on an outermost branch.
I look for it everywhere.
Above us the 40th Street Bridge
full of stalled commuters heading home.
Above them a few inland seagulls
dreaming about the ocean maybe.
Above them, if you have the right glasses,
Venus passing in front of the Sun.

TOAD

Thumb among the crumpled things
underfoot, hind legs folded up
in leopard stripes, tiny
front hands pigeon-toed.
Warted as wet leather.
Leaping between stones
and snakes, into leaf-ceilinged rooms
within the fallen, flecked-with-mold world,
another stone with eyes, tense,
pebbled back bent on disguise.
Do I really need another body?
Why then do I pick him up?

THE APPLICANT

Do you put your penis in every poem?
Why or why not? Make your reasoning rhyme.

How many times have you given up on words?
In the course of your life? This year? Today?

What was the first noun that found its way back?
What one verb do you wish had remained lost?

By what right does a change begin? What's left after?
Please refrain from using "happily" as an answer.

How does your garden grow? Who is your animal
named for? On which side does he sleep at night?

Christopher Phelps

Alone in a Closed System

ARISTOPHANES, IF NOT HALVES

We were keys to one another, which meant

We were keyholes to one another, which meant
We were keys with keyholes in ourselves—

Alone in one closed system, completeness

Was perfectly out of reach—
In another

Perfectly tempting

TWO OF A KIND

What if Narcissus were heard
Not by Echo
That hapless bird
Humming out of league

But by a second plucky boy—
Two languors of light caught like
The wan in want, the shallow grin
Of an infinity mirror, sure

We story happiness not to stay
With those who look too close—
Alone in a closed system
Peeking through our jalousies

With binoculars, adjusting
To the manifest of nectar—
The möbius of beauty
Turning on itself

DAO(T)

By time he knew the way, he knew the way
Wasn't the way—

Alone in a closed system,
Right as three left turns—he couldn't take

The leftovers home
Because that would be evidence—

It was easy for me to nail a string to the wall
And call it art and call it difficult

So I used the hammer's end
We hear less about, curved and composed

To take the nail out, to let the string be
As it was—strong, stranded—holding on to paint

I loved as long as error—eros as a rose
Petaling under water, reaching the surface hungry

NOBODADDY

Jeffrey Dahmer blamed "the lie" of evolution—
That we came from slime and when we die
"That's it"—

Alone in a closed system

A brain with its desires—
How could one go wrong
When there's no two?

Filling the frontal lobes

With acid, holes drilled in their heads
To keep these handsome creatures
Alive, in the narrowest sense, his

Body, surrounded by body—

In the end, lacking "avenues,"
He opened up, settled into prison life—
Courteously reconciled with his father

Jesus, always perfectly fresh

From the distance of redemption
Carved at the joints, dehisced:
This is my body broken for you

ALONE IN A CLOSED SYSTEM

There was only one beautiful side of your skin—

There was only one beautiful side of your skin?
Underneath was a thick weepy network of unknowns—

Proxy-fight or transcendence-twisted?—

Without transgression, your naked body
Looked perfect to me—still

Perfectly clothed to me

RECURSION

1

The house animals
Look at us again

With their Rilkean awareness,
Which is to say, awareness

No name can claim
While we disclaim

Feed after brush,
Sweep after rush,

We are not your gods—
But it sounds all the same

Clang, the same hanging
Query mark to brains

Without language to press on
What reads as a question

2

Could it be the same again
With our curious noise

Offered up-ankle
To the invisible: god knows

If god knows or hears or cares
To exist, our love torn up, the dish

Of milk willfully spilled,
The dash into walls,

The misspellings most of all
Of *wrist* and *wisk*, *good* and *ghost*,

As *risk* and *wish*, *god* and *host*, wondering
Would words ever be right?—

Alone in a closed system
We say, they seem

CONVENTIONAL WISDOM

On the way to old age, to make it
You'd better look like a skeleton

Hide in plain sight
And meet your end by degrees—

Was this true, and if true
Was it worth being true?

The deep breath of baking pizza crust
On the long run: the one song

That is enough and not enough—
Infinitely good / enough, I wonder—

To last suggests an ending, an ending
Suggests something still in process—

A bending back, looking back
I saw you two passengers in one seat

Kissing at a stop sign—
I kept running like I had a route

But here I am, still out on a limb
Toe-holding a little Malebranche

To think what makes us up
Moment-to-moment

Isn't momentum—isn't atoms or energy—
Isn't God so named and overnamed

But mystery reclaimed from skeleton keys—
A better idol, an icon we may have classed

But can't be broken if we're to last—
The earth, alone in a closed system?—

Its tensions allowed to be reverberatory
Lovers, tenuous and strenuous

Alike, transverse-pliable like
A sinusoidal wave

Made of reversals—rehearsals forward—
One way or another a spiral is progress?

The circle is broken? The kiss is planted—
The run is finished—The night opens up

To the sky, its prize won and unwinnable
As a backdrop, as a showcase fretwork

CHRISTOPHER PHELPS

MOTION MACHINE

Sedentary: cemetery: allies for a reason
That life is in motion means
Rest means death, and yet

A kinetic sculpture like this one
On the upper floor of Logan Airport
Calms in its turns and trickles—
Its xylophonic tweets and claves—
Its rubber balls, bearings in no hurry

To be a clock: It is not
Meant to mean delay: It is not
Encouragement to worry: It is us

Alone in a closed system, with guidelines
We made for Sisyphus, this time to play
At highest ape, this looking glass as-if
A view, this motor lift and roller feat
Within this luggage-handled pause

Collective, then
Collected into queue—
The pattern of our chosen straws—

GEGENSCHEIN

The sky still slowly rolls
Its tongue around the melting cube

The wandering photons minstrels
Of a tall true tale called
The Big Bang: unlike most makings
It seems there was no delay

Between seed and bud
Between bud and bloom

No delay between milk and egg
The oven infinitely hot
The cake baked on conception
Our virgin birth from quantum foam

Uncanny-quiet, the universe
Just now, as now goes

About to accelerate its
Expansion faster and faster
So fast that someday light
Will not connect us

Island to island all
Lost on ourselves

The archipelago shrunk
From a body of burning stars
To ours and only hours
We're just quick enough

To have discovered being
Followed up its trick

With a flight from the scene
Of what worked as the word as
Speed is what an airplane needs
To be a human bird

In its catch and keep: you may
Hold on while we accelerate

It will be over in a moment's
Hungry, lonely closure—line by line
Grove by grove, now by now
A window view, some gegenschein

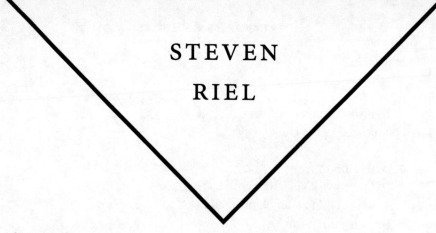

STEVEN RIEL

selections from

13 WAYS OF LOOKING AT MY EFFEMINANCY

& other poems

POSTCARD FROM P-TOWN

How could I not write to you here?
Ramshackle floorboards, painted lullaby-blue,
creak underfoot. You'd notice plaster-soft wood,
hollowed treads, guess at olden layers of gloss.
Up on the second floor, we're making a nest,
striding across rooms & rooms of bumpy sky!
Walls: butter-yellow. Woodwork: clean white.
We've opened every window to its screen.
Bird-chirps & breeze swirl through our tree house.
One side peers over a bower of wisteria—
I am not making this up, dear!—
benches placed, dream-like, for tête-à-têtes,
while heavy-headed dahlias nod—& I must mention
a truck just rattled the length of town,
delivering something wanted. How could I not
wish you were here?

THE TEACUP I DESIRE

The pattern of teacup I desire
depicts bouquets of mauve roses
tied together by just-picked violets.
Once tea's poured out, a sipping
striptease could reveal thorn
by thorn, as Earl Grey eases
down the length of stem,
at last unveiling unopened buds,
their inviting scents
glazed beneath sugar sediments.

To lift this flowery
vessel in my hands,
to walk it to the cashier, & blushing
or not, to state, *I'd like this,*
would draw a noticeable dot
out where it could be
connected.

        If I begin to collect
teacups (not to mention matching
tea trays, sugar bowls, creamers),
ownership might imply the swan-like
curve in this cup's handle
replicates a sway in my soul,
how I'd arch my arms out of
a thin sweater if I were a starlet
at some Hollywood supper—but naturally
the indelible dots would have proliferated by then,
cups & cups & cups' worth: upside-down tulip skirts
fit for Marie Antoinette & *moi*;
angle-handled Art Decos

in lozenge-like crackle
leaning forward to chat at a café—

                                            Might this step towards
one schoolmarmish cup unlatch all
the knickknacks that polka-dot my mind:
salt & pepper sets of every bent & hue
dishing each other across what-not shelves
lining stairs that spiral turret-high
in my dreams—grasshopper-motif bric-à-brac,
amber brooches, blue Nancy Drews,
buttons like peppermints, scroll-handled keys. . . .

An obedient boy, forbidden his own stuffed animal,
sits on the edge of his sister's bed
when he finds himself alone. Eventually
his sweaty palm pets not the velvet,
but the shadow of her dog—

yes—honeybee heads for the rose it wants,
shoves proboscis into clenched blossoms,
rubs hairy forelegs into pollen
to pack its perfect honeycomb. The gold
splash on my teacup's handle
mirrors me back as a small dot
that's now part of its pattern.

CRAYOLA CRUELLA

I came of age during one of those crafty
seven-year pauses Disney places between releases,
but didn't need the movie to sweep me away,
or even its trailer to tease me.
All it took was a cheap coloring book,
typical spin-off Hollywood cranks out
to puff profits, displayed to catch
the doe-eye of a soft-spoken boy
who would wend down dime-store aisles.
Once I had my prize safely home,
its newsprint pages lying soft beneath my palm,
I grasped the reason for that
white crayon in every pack
as I waxed in her opposing hair-slash,
highlighted its shock of black.

Instead of a broom, Cruella had glamour—
the nasty kind. The base
of her phone cradled its handset with claws;
pink cigarettes spat smoke
at the tip of her swank holder;
her jade alligator lighter
blazed red eyes each time it was stoked;
& she had a checkbook;
& she had Hell Hall;
& she had thieves at her beck & call—

so I silvered slit-eyes
of her purring Panther coupe,
blackened in points of ermine tails,
darkened peach within concave curves
of her skeletal cheekbones & shins—

my boy-eyes in a town too tiny for a drive-in,
mind's eye open, a ready pond
reflecting livid lightning bolts
or a coloring book's surging sketches—
"Imbeciles, get to the crossroads!
Head off those puppies!" I'd shriek,
unleashing the cackle within.

LENA HORNE

i. She Watches Herself: 1960

I knocked back two martinis before
flipping on the set to catch myself.
These are the openings I've smoldered for.
Now that I've wedged my Viviered toe
back inside the sound-stage door,
the drop-dead half of a duet with Frank,
Dixieland's shears can't snip me out.
Today's houses have antennas.
MGM kept me out of the story
so the plot would splice nice if I were gone.
I have cause to dwell on it.
Sure, I would have stuck
in Tuscaloosa's craw. My Grandmother Horne
was the bastard of a gray-eyed Calhoun.
I'm not girl enough to think my curv-
aceous strut on tonight's ABC
will save the balls of my brothers
backed into some mud-rutted hollow, but
it's being broadcast from Newark to Yalobusha,
& I'm digging my Hope Diamond grin
'cause I'm about to let 'em have it
with just how smooth this "Negress"
in a thousand-dollar spangle can swing.

ii. I Watch You: 2005

Clicking past public TV,
I arrow back till I marvel, face to face
with—Who's *she*? At first I see only the sparkle
of fitted obsidian gown: mermaid at midnight.
Then you open your piano-wide mouth into yawning
indifference, curl a lip
around a lament, scorch an ex
with a blaze in the onyx of your eyes.
The only humans I've encountered
this aquiver with drama
are drag queens, who glue themselves together
follicle by mannerism by phrase.
They strive to disappear
as they reveal a diva.
My stare is stuck
to every quirky nod & glare
as you mix sadness & seduction
like gasoline & fire, cooing, coaxing,
Don't you wanna forget someone, too?
while Sinatra, overdue for a vacation,
goes through the motions,
abstractedly snapping his fingers
next to a live one.

iii. Song Stylist

Days later, biographies
fanned like feathers on my bed,
I'm puzzling out your sorrows,
trying on their contours.
They say people paid to see you,
not to hear you sing.
But your half of this duet I gawked at
aired eons after your debut
as jailbait at the Cotton Club.
By the Sixties, you'd been blacklisted,
breathed freedom in France,
left off leaning against pedestals,
crooning in a vacant vibrato
to no one in particular—
tutored by your new husband, now
each word came flavored, drenched
in style. Was this success,
or a thick after-dinner drink
for those smoky clubs in Vegas?
In my mirror, I'm
overlaying the outlines,
asking me asking you asking me:
Who sang instead of us?
What were we expecting:
revolution? Was it too late;
had the damage been done;
did just another act
upstage the song?

CRUISING, POST-MODERN STYLE
A PARODY THAT RESISTED

(Or like a den tucked from headlights—
dun path perhaps leading to—no, flushing out—
nothing but a cul-de-sac, its own doubling
back. Not a maze this time, no jerked neck
when whispers ooze where dew cools,
when a big one unrolls a condom
against incisor-white roots
where tendrils steady hollow stalks.

                                  A phalanx
of invasives rattled by a stiff wind
hasn't a prayer of barring your way.
As if you lived here. As if you planned
how semen glistens & might light your mission,
as if being told) not only
(*that a parting might unfold.*
Or has. Why not begin to heed
how pocketed keys rearrange their jab,
or even how memory convinces through stench,
how toilet-tissue litter waits for rain

                                    to give in
to mire, its—necessity?—almost grasped
when a denizen borrows incandescence or maybe
moonlight. One or the other might uncloak
gum-line of root-nub, the whites of eyes,
grotto where sneakers resemble loaves
&—this is where you genuflect—mud is a crust
adhering to that unveiling you hunt
& all that's shadowed to glimpse it:

thorn, handcuff, altar) *not only.*

STEVEN RIEL

WALKING BEHIND TENNYSON AT CAUTERETZ
HENRY GRAHAM DAKYNS, 1861

All along the valley I stall ten yards behind,
not wishing to distract a grief much rawer still than mine.
All along the valley I will not blurt, *I knew.*
I will not try your confidence. I will not breathe, *Me, too.*

Since Hallam never fancied your frank grin as you hoped
(pale hip glowing milkily; bedsheet lifted, mute),
all along this valley, undress before "What then?"

(Ahh . . .
Many a coal sighs low, no tinder tempting blaze.)

Never a deeper sorrow could anchor in your soul,
never another unkissed mouth unnestle all you fold.
Never another donkey ride to ponder what you shared
alongside what you didn't, because your sister did.

Never before you die will you be followed by such as me
who fingers clues of avalanche on every stone and tree.
All along the valley I hear you mumble low,
but let you rein, reverse, converse with echoes long ago.
All along the valley, bloom and stem pressed tight,
I tuck my gift inside my book—don't trouble thee with sight.

WHITE DIAMONDS
A PERFUME COMMERCIAL

High-stakes poker in a black and white resort.
Prequel: grand entrances. First: stacked
goddess flirts with attendant paparazzi;
next: Adonis disembarks down tarmac *escalier*.
Backdrop: oasis with its desert horizon. Swaying
palm fronds, billowing sheers that beckon
and hint at pharaoh-sized beds, baths, unguents,
fragrant cotton. Mythic tryst. White buck of a god's
unbuttoned, as yet unfingered, silk.

Save him. So you can have him.
The Isis in you intervenes.

Not so fast, Von Ryan,
you warn, in a carefully careless drawl
that veils its lurking growl. Reputation:
the fastest woman in the known world,
whose flames the Vatican's mouthpiece deigns to condemn.
News flash: unrepentant.

These have always brought me luck:
on the table you toss many-carat clip-ons.
Easy come, easy go. Cleopatra's pearl dissolved,
a wager cheap vinegar won by eating away.
What are gems or vows to a velvet purr—
what is luck when heaven blesses with savage cleavage,
double-rowed lashes framing amethyst eyes—
Go ahead, Marc Antony, throw the dice.

PHOTOGRAPH OF A SURVIVOR

Like a somnambulant camel,
he drags across the chalky land,
past corpses of those fallen
to famine or plague.
Bodies half-buried by shifting sands,
their tibias like tent poles pitch
the most concave cadavers imaginable.
Numbly he yanks a thread of strength
to lift his feet, puppet-like,
from out of the swallowing dune;

would we ask him to kneel in the grit
to mourn classmates, his baby sister?
He cannot spare the water for tears,
so intent is he on the possibility
that the wake of beige dust
drawn along by the van
with sacks of cornmeal and sorghum
might be scanned from the ridge
beyond the one that wavers before him.

JACKSON SABBAGH

Fall from Your Hands

OCD PROVERBS

1. You tuck the blankets tight under your toes. (Tighter. Tighter—
2. In darkness the will eyes dilate.
3. Tadpoles go ugly—swim in their scat. Flit in stillwater
    to its nonexistent source.
4. Tighter
4. Tighter.
4Too tight.)

5. Before God—there was this darkness.

6. Like a geyser's breath, swatting the air, sunlight pushes down on the floor like a bad lover, which is easy.
7. You are reminded of being reminded. —Your incredible feet.
8. (You will chew, tug, then clip at your nails.)
9. Shovel the thought into the alleged pit.
10. Two clouds pass by, doing nothing.

PRAYER FOR WARMTH

The knuckles go cold, clasped
in their prayer for warmth.

His answer is no   where in the fishnet of stars;
and, sick of each other's pallid glow,

still the fingers touch in an unweatherable knot
like atoms at the tucked core of iceberg.   No

hummed God—no warmth.   Why don't you pray
for *cold*—   *more* cold—   I like it

when you respect the world's patterns.
     One time (He bragged)   I watched five John

Malkovich films in a weekend.   Patterns smooth over
the heart   give the brain X & Y   coordinate

to bound freely inside.   You're cold, little
one? then clasp those cold Hands   and pray

for cold Feet to match!   He boomed on,
Leave the groom at the altar   for all I care!

     Tears underscored His eyes.

He cleared His throat: If I got cold feet
on *my* Wedding Day, I would say— *hey*

I registered for *frankincense!*
     God leaned back and sniffled

at his bad joke.   His voice went low:
Listen. When you pray for *warmth*—hope,

a flaming grapefruit perched   on the sky
          Open

the window. Go to bed as the room chills.
Whatever happens—you opened the window

for Me.   I'm not the certainty
you need—   to which, like a Proverb,

or a gold standard, you can   *Transmogrify.*
Calvin and Hobbes,   He said fondly,

loved the cold—they prayed for snow to fall
as it was snowing down. They found their Theme:

restlessness. Find yours. My theme is the only thing
I have to be: God, God, God.

JACKSON SABBAGH

HOW MANY TIMES YOU FOLLOW LOVE

1

You fear becoming late.
Despite this, you stop your car on the overpass
and love
and you do become late.

2

Stationed at the desk, you're pinched
by doubt: a familiar feeling
of being tripped by a stone that isn't
there. —Then you ignore it:
you lean your pen into the love.

3

At midnight you love it. At noon
you lose it.
It would've been so easy—
if you had nothing and no one
and just had to love
the trees.
Now, you have nothing, so look
at the trees.

4

At your TV, you stare; a kind of love:
your heart syncs up with the evening
news. If this is real,
what you're doing, then the news has to be

real. A bomb story breaks
but the world only bends.

5

You check the mailbox:
nothing. When is love
supposed to come? Are you searching for it
wrong
in the hotel mirror: to close up
or too close
to the hot shower's reign?

6

You can't help but laugh: you always knew
you were a maverick. He revs the engine
for a leonine sound: your hands come round
his belly like a prayer.
Your brother can wait . . .
your future can wait . . .
he swerves the motorcycle left, into the sunrise
which is gorging down its mouth on the highway
like a grandfather's lips to his inhaler.

7

In a reststop bathroom,
the gray floor marked with blue and red:
you curl against the wall;
you sink down, breathing in the solitude.
—Then your voice intervenes: *You are. You are. You are.*

8

You open your umbrella—this is the way to love

the rain. You listen for the pre-storm chickadees:
this is the way to love
complete silence.

9

He pours you a glass of California Red
from the year 2000. You remember: there are 2000
red blood cells in one mouth. You feel blood
rush to your head, then a cathartic image—
the reststop wall.

10

Your stomach's a black hole;
your mind's a gas tank in the car chase for OJ.
As you walk the roadside,
pillow feathers
from your first love
fall from your hands.

11

You are late for something
that happens in your family. Death,
the funeral.
You were writing, that's why;
you were writing about love.

12

Most of all you love
the pale, idly-glowing convenience
store cashier. Under the counter:
you kiss his small mouth, needing it,
even the semicolon of acne

which pauses his cheek.
And you say *Twelve* in your head, which makes
a surge of guilt. Why are you counting love?
His open-mouth kiss pushes you
into the Snickers rack,
and you can't think anymore—
so you don't,
which is Almighty Love.

SERIES OF BIRTHS

I was welcomed from the midwife's womb
by blue jays, deer, and the people taking it well:
watching *me*, the subject of *subject-and-verb* fame.

*

A cartoonist drew me on the sky.
The clouds were my speech bubbles. Post-Missouri
humor was self-aware in that way.

*

She has me on the emerald, freshly-mowed grass
of Derek's pool table's felt. Three of his friends walk in—
cocks, common as carbon—and talk mental health.

*

I was born as the chapter of an 80's high school
novel began. The video arcade gleams
its lemonade novas. A concrete skate-park

re-directs wind with its mouth.

*

I watched from the floor: the whole world
being perceived by a terminally-ill waitress
as a triumphantly-aureate Dali; by the boy she served,

a terminally-ill waitress.

INVENTORY OF MEN

1

Like a skunk, a sudden block of the sidewalk,
you turned me around for a new way home:
I strayed
into a shadowy rivulet of the map.

We kissed first
on a side-street of life-sized dollhouses, federal
oak trees symbolizing the woods;
a branch-level snake of yellow lighting
glowed on us (the city planner
alluding to astrology).

    We pulled away
at the clank: a skunk, sifting the garbage:
throned in a mess of peels, filters,
shells; he looked at us in hope
of satisfaction. His eyes were two halves
of a split black pearl—virginal, irrelevant.

We ran off in a giddy handhold—
I turned back where the skunk sat—
he was a crisp black-and-white
like the film version   of *A Streetcar Named Desire*
in which Stanley tears the pearls
straight from the neck.

2

After our date, you came home.
Your cock—swollen by vein—
ivy, climbing the Washington—
it loomed in my whole vision—
wavering like a steady gas flame—
generated for fuel.

As I sucked its length down, then up, your toady
hands wrapped in my hair, rippled the marble
fat by the roots: oafish, drawled,
a disenchantment of the swanlike.

The surface
crashed all ways in the glass:
as the morning folded
I fed water to your lip.
You left soon after,
but in the poems
to come, the speaker brought milk
to your lip
every morning—each time
I read it, the morning.

In one, I squeezed the milk my-
self from a farm cow resting in the grass.
The sun rose relentlessly
like a hole bore into the sky's throat
by hot cigars.

3

Cowboys never tell
who they love—

nor why it happens
indoors.

A cowboy is seen
standing where the dust diffuses:
the street's clapboard houses
a still audience on every side.
Facing him
a townie, young, but a heart's
all he has to lose.

A dark revolver, hilted and packed,
is the outermost boundary
of both men. And if there's love
in the cowboy, as the sun revolves
his wrist might flinch

as he thinks to surrender
in kindness or for morale.

Moonlight lays bright ethers on the matchwood porches.
The air plots with the smell of whiskey-breath
and passing tumbleweed.
I might love you

the townie says,
a click clearing his throat.
The cowboy, forced by his name
to draw, hesitates—a nod to love—
then raises it, nimble: his expertise.

From what I've seen,
if God ain't hot for you,
that ain't God.

ONE DIRECTION

These cherubs drop pianissimo
from a cloud in a slow downward spiral,
and sing about nothing.
Their hair, brown and windswept as
a tractor-clipped barley field,
is lit by the sun, giving the stray hairs
an echo. I feel hope; wherever I was before,
I'm not there anymore.
They dangled from the arena ceiling:
five doves shaped from thin quartz and hung
on the strings of a mobile
wearing the sunshine o'er me. One

cannot embody hope—
but hope shivers in you, an heirloom,
primitive thanks: flares, or almost flares
in the graze of two boys' swinging hands
against each other, breaking the Boundary.

Wind from the hands of hopeless girls
sends smaller hands of wind through the loose hair
of these boys: breath through a dying bonfire.

My warning to all the other infants:
use hope
sparingly, like ice cream.
If not, the apple trees grow bare,
your nails erode from the citrus.
Groupies look up into the abyss
which is the 2 AM sky
above the cars as they exit the doors.

JACKSON SABBAGH

Try swimming
far, far out
into the night water by your house.
The sea is grave, and always black,
and unlike the boys, your plunged body
writes its own music.

BURGLAR

Even my doubt
was theirs.
I heard their ice cubes
melting
in the freezer.
Yesterday's hour
read on the cuckoo clock.

I watched a movie
in their living room. (I watched
movies
for mimicry.) Blanche DuBois
was easy
to mimic, her whole life
being a mimicry
of grace.

I poured a small
bit of Wild Turkey.
I tried
to drink it
inevitably,
like Berryman:
at the study window
I stared down on a
puddle
quicksilvered in the gravel.

The whiskey
grew warm, Massachusetts.

Blanche put her hand on the doorknob,
breathed in,
and entered Massachusetts.

ROBERT WHITEHEAD

Bad Prophets

HISTORY

WITH LINES FROM ANNE CARSON'S *NOX*

To leave behind a memory (costume morning when he told me, put on whatever song) or monument (whatever song you want) at once concrete and indecipherable (the light the rest of the world rejected was in us) a storydog that roams (as the song rose into its terror) bits of muteness (love me love me say you do) referring not to silence (each pitched bottle in the bin marking our joy) but to a certain fundamental opacity (as a swift joy) of human being (certain passage into which away would come for us next) as swans drift down the water (he was in his costume, dancing and throwing the bottles) into the muteness (and I was singing the song because I meant it) he refuses (or wanted to mean it) at once monument (to a someone he could have been) and silence (who was good, as the river we watched once was good) the overtakelessness, under a wide thin sorrowful sky (until we got in and found it was divine).

RAPTURE IN THE MIDST OF A FLAGGING DANCE
FOR RICKEY LAURENTIIS

As if a man fighting with a white iris big as his body.
Or fighting the robes of a fluent angel. He had a flag
for both his hands, made each belong to a billowing,
made the air around him unsettle like a mane of a lost horse.
He had broken through the blueprint installed on the night
and now measured, with a surge of edges, a new problem.
Like an augur, he interpreted two wings of the same violence
inside the music, inside the promise of the music.
The rest of the room was irrelevant. Every eye was on him.
It had been so long since we'd seen something pure.
A blue light hounded after where he spun, a scattering
of greens saying O. If he seemed to be in trouble, we had no way
to get to him, and he did seem in trouble. When the music ended
and he let go the neck of what can be gorgeous,
he was changed—tyranny a tusk in him, his marauded look.
He shined like a glacier. The freaked battalion of his flags he folded
into his pocket, looking out at us like an eye seeing the sun.
Then he touched us and told us with his touch
                        everything helpless he had learned.

ROBERT WHITEHEAD

I
IS A
VANITY
IN EVERY
WAY, WHICH
DOES NOT MEAN
BEAUTY IN A BALL
MIRROR, IS NOT WHAT
SETS THE MILLION SHIPS
SAILING. IT'S SURVIVAL, SIR,
AND I INTENDED TO DO IT FOR A
SOFT WRIST OR THIGH A BLUE EYE
A WISE LOOK IN THE SHOWER DOOR
REFLECTING AN EXACT REPLICA OF MY
GHOST. AN OPINION IS JUST A PLACE WHERE
YOUR OWN NATURE HAS DAMAGED YOU & I'VE
GOT A MILLION OPINIONS. IS IT ANY WONDER THE
LARGEST PLANET HAS THE MOST WEATHER OR THAT
IN EGYPT THEY ALWAYS FELL IN LOVE WITH ONE SIDE OF
A FACE. DIDN'T THEY MAKE A LANGUAGE OUT OF FIGURES,
LEAVING BEHIND THE FIRST GREAT RECORD OF WHAT VANITY
CAN ACCOMPLISH. A HORNED VIPER SIGNIFIED POSSESSION, OWLS
FACED THE ONE WHO DREW THEM. INVITATIONS WERE ONLY ON THE
INNER WALLS FOR THE DEAD TO ANSWER. TO FURNISH A PERFECT LACK.

ROBERT WHITEHEAD

A
RED
SUN SO
DARING IT
MUST SPELL
EITHER DANGER
OR GOOD FORTUNE.
I READ IN SOME BOOK
MATTER & VOID ARE THE
ONLY REALITIES, ANYTHING
ELSE IS OPINION. I THINK I READ
WE ARE ALWAYS ON THE VERGE OF
A DRASTIC END OR A PERFECTION. I'LL
DO ONE BETTER : NO ABSOLUTE WILL SET
A BLUE FOOT ON THIS PLANET. AS A TACTIC,
LANGUAGE WORKS BUT IT'S THE ONLY WAY WE
HAVE TO SAY HOW ONCE A SUN GOT SHOCK RED
& STAYED OUT ALL NIGHT ASKING WHERE AM I? HOW
I CAME TO ON A FLOOR OF SOME SLEEPING BOY'S ROOM
AND ASKED AND ASKED INSIDE THE ROOM'S SILENCE WHILE
I GATHERED MY CLOTHES TO LEAVE. THE FUTURE TENSE MADE
ME BELIEVE IN BAD PROPHETS, THE PRESENT THAT I AIM TOWARD
WONDER. I READ SOMEWHERE THAT THE PAST IS UNALTERABLE. BUT
THE SUN STAYED SUMMITED. I SAID I WANTED THE BOY & I MADE IT TRUE.

ROBERT WHITEHEAD

                              I
                             WAS
                           A CHILD
                          NOW I AM
                         A CHILD. THE
                         CURSE OF MYTH
                        IS TRANSFORMING
                       INVISIBLY & THERE'S
                      THE STORY OF YOUR LIFE.
                     I AM A CHILD BECAUSE MANY
                   THINGS ARE, TO ME, IMPOSSIBLE.
                  WHEN THE HEAVENS LAID ME DOWN
                 IT WAS INTO A GOODBYE LAND, A LOSS.
                WHEN THE TITANIC SUNK THE SEA NEVER
               LOOKED THE SAME. AS WHEN ROME LOST ITS
              HEAD & SAT DOWN WAITING TO DIE. ONLY THAT
             PEOPLE GRIEVED DID I KNOW SOMETHING BAD WAS
            HAPPENING. A NEW UNBEARABLE SEASON. THEY TOLD
           THE STORY SO MANY TIMES, I EVENTUALLY BELIEVED IT :
          CHAOS RULED ALL, THEN ORDER, THEN CHAOS AGAIN. OUR
         EMPEROR REMOVED HIS BLOOD-RED CLOAK TO BURN IT IN ONE
        OF THE MANY NEW FIRES. IT WAS A SYMBOL : I'VE GIVEN ALL THAT
       I KNEW TO GIVE & I HAVE NO STRENTH LEFT. I ENTERED THE WRONG
      PLACE & STAYED. I WAS A VAGRANT CHILD, THIS WAS NEVER MY DREAM.

ROBERT WHITEHEAD

BUT YOU NEVER TOLD ME ABOUT THE FIRE

The one blue light of the bathhouse buzzed as we
approached. You were shaking when

you said a need is truer than a want
so I asked, *What do you need?*

A latch lifted in you and a stranger entered.
The stranger said, *I need to be wanted.*

A traffic of hands most brute to behold
made use of you. You wanted to but could not

stop them. *To apply oneself takes a work of rapture*,
you said, like a stranger to desire. Like a martyr to it.

I tended to you as I would a man on the threshold.
I tried moving like you, flame-ward into the strange place.

This is the strange place, I told you
and you made me a house there.

Further into the night, the bathhouse men
were seen without any disguises.

They were fucking not the stranger in you
but the one most impenetrable NO they could conjure.

They were alone on the planet of their want.
They gave you nothing but a wind filling you

then turning away. You said, *the complete I
only comes out of hiding when ransomed.*

It takes any door in hand and runs throwing out
its arms. Overhead the supernova kindled.

You, a fox with your red tail and I,
the one always after you. The men looked up

from the edge of their work and hushed,
astonished. A desert of blue started shaking

in each of us. The text of the spectacle read,
a vision of a single black petal upon which

two figures practiced one direction of a dance.
Come dance with me, fox. Come, stranger.

MOTH ON WATER

A rescue would be out of the question. The moth's dust wings
were transparent if not robbed. The moth flitted in the water
until it could only float, ready for it. Then the boy sailors called
from under their dropped sails and if I knew what was best
I would meet their parish with two calm hands. Distraction
is as sacred as dreaming is to moths who do not dream. Sacred
as the image of the water, still as glass, and my memory
making a flagrant boat of the moth, going down. The forest
lost a million moths in a century. This was just another.
And still I couldn't hold it out to the flint night. Imagine the risks,
showing exactly how ruined one beauty can become in the wade
of another. After they were through with me, the sailors would
petrify from the astonishing anger required to reach me.
But still, they always called back. Perhaps they forgot
how they turned nacre-eyed, turned away from themselves,
diminished. Or perhaps it was a part of why they returned.
The moth was an emblem carrying some element of the sailors
who tried to captain this unraveling within them and failed
each time. I wouldn't walk past the docks for weeks after
a visit. Until I was sure the sailors needed me again. Until
I thought they could double for billows with all their empty.
If the boys risked something it wasn't something of mine.
I surrendered all my feelings, I let them take me like drowning.
If the boys and I agreed on one thing it was this : nothing
would come to harm without first wanting it.

ROBERT WHITEHEAD

TO BEAR THE YOKE

We have been with the wild horses of your worry
standing still in the fog. We have been seaside

when the sea mistranslated how still you could stand
for something about certainty
                                  and knocked you down.

We have a secret : you're not the only one struggling.
There's a tribe of us, like work horses in the fog,

like gathered marigolds in the hand of the man
with a bluer eye for ruin.
                        We all have that man.

He rides the horses to hurt them. He is the waves, knocking.
You have been managing but it is a tough job.

No fog lifts without making way for more weather.
A secret sea must inhabit you.
                              A grammar which cannot

translate to a tamer animal. You must position yourself
as if you've been working. You hold on as you must.

EMANUEL XAVIER

Want and Struggle

RED

Everyone you have ever truly been in love with
Every moment you have feared for your life—
something punishable by law or a society of oppression

Every time you want to scream,
to hold him or her in your arms
to protect them from the world around you

Same as two becoming one
that one love that is the same love
the sameness of two in love

Born free to be told who to be
shaped to fill
an acceptable mold

Your heart belongs to the revolution
Your heart must be contained
Your heart is not your own

Love is to be determined
Love is to be preached
and love is why they destroy

Children should not be exposed
God will not return as long
as they continue to love the same

Pain and suffering
will not end
until they do

It is time for them to die
It is time for demons to retreat
It is time for humiliation

I have fallen in love with your beautiful Russian men
muscular   feeding hunger   hardworking fathers
watching sunsets   learning cultures   drinks   music

I imagined myself a lover   lost   in your language
a wardrobe of coats   a warm embrace against my body
searching for poetic translations and lineage of history

I too have survived remaining distant and misunderstood
the villainous, untrustworthy spy
thoughts of socialism and a radical too

In New York City, my Russian lover holds my hand
on the subway all the way from Brighton Beach
because he can and does not care that people stare

He knows that even here we could be killed
unwelcome to appear as anything more than
two men traveling together, no public displays of affection allowed

A Russian man guns us down with the contempt in his eyes
Back home, our body bags would be spat upon
shame that someone from his country has been tainted

not by an American per se, but worse, a minority
All we share in common is being other
left to the fringes of distant cities

raised to believe in sin and documentation
rent   bills   procreation
devastation   government

It is only winters that we understand
harsh winds
hats   gloves

I have been beaten by strangers,
my own kind, non-Soviet
on our own U.S. pavements

I have been left out in the cold
for dead to go to hell
without bus fare

The same moon that shines for us all—my guidance
shining bright for sisters and brothers
regardless of what is natural or unnatural

offering light to darkness and predators
How do we boycott the sun?
How many wars must be waged against nature?

When do damaged children find salvation?
Is this same love a new thing to the world?
Can all those who think differently be destroyed?

If spirits walk the earth, some of them have loved too and heaven
perhaps   is crowded   with dead lovers   odd aunts
strange uncles   men with breasts   women confused for boys

and loneliness   but mostly   want
and struggle   seemingly   only belongs
to color   religion   race   creed   politics

countries of angry teens and adults (not children)
countries of guns and altars
a country of men?

Where will the perverts be buried? When will they stop
being born? Why do they plague every corner of this earth?
Jamaica? Uganda? Puerto Rico?

On this day it is the loved
and loving that must bleed
and those who speak openly about love

they will turn the sky red
after they are all gone
and the world will be the same

GOLDEN SHOWER AT A MOTEL 6 IN SAN ANTONIO

It is quite unexpected.
He is extremely drunk.
Sexy body. Pretty boy
Mexican. He comes back
to my room at the Motel 6,
French kissing in the cab.
I'm surprised he doesn't mama bird
me in the back seat. It is too late
to send him home.
We undress.
I figured we could cuddle
all night long in each other's arms
before morning sex.
Comfort from a recent break up.
We mess around naked.
Fall asleep like long time lovers.
In the middle of the night,
I smell a foul stench in the air.
With the bathroom only
a few feet away,
his urine soaks
into the sheets, wetness
creeps toward my legs, he giggles.
I have willingly enjoyed
a playful piss from a lover
in the shower as an act of love.
Perhaps I've participated
in water sports with kinky men.
But I have never had anyone
pull a #1 while laying
next to me in some cheap motel.

He continues to sleep.
I stare at the ceiling horrified.
If he was embarrassed,
he simply casually moves
the stained bedsheets to the side,
embraces me.
In his twenties, he is too old
for diapers. Too young for medical
issues. Waking him up seems
foolish. Yes, I don't want to
shame him or shove his face
into the yellowed fabric
to train him like my cat.
I wonder if he still expects
me to suck him off
when the sun comes up.
Tomorrow, I'll call him Pee Diddy!
I'm afraid to think what 'getting
shit-faced' might mean in his universe.
Will he tell his friends?
I am now sleepless
with the thought of having been dumped
and then literally pissed on.
I would be the one to pick up
the guy with bladder problems
who can't control his flow.
This was supposed to be
about connecting with another man—
one who wore big boy pants.
It's a good thing I've slept through
several interesting situations.
I eventually drift off—
awakening to find him staring
down at me. He is hungry
and goes down. My cock
responds dutifully as my eyes

search for the crumpled, tossed
victim. I want to grab my cell
and phone-a-friend but he might
notice. For all of his hard work,
I can't cum. We chit chat instead,
he gets quickly dressed, I call him
a cab. We never mention it—the
smelly Big Bird in the room.
We kiss and hug to seal the moment.
It's a bittersweet goodbye, perhaps
more bitter than sweet—the kind soldiers
give each other while dead bodies
rot just a few feet away.
What will the cleaning lady think?
I guess I'll have to tip her well.
I worry she'll think it was me—
an adult guest staying at a Motel 6,
near a pool, fresh, clean toilet,
dirty laundry—soaked with minerals—
a little boy scared of the dark.

STEP FATHER

He forgets that he used to call me *mariconcito*—
that I harbored years of hatred toward him
while hoping to find my real father. My
childhood memories of him reminding me
I was my mother's son, not his. I tried
to poison him once and scattered sharp nails
inside the shoes in his closet. By the time one
of his sons died of AIDS, I was already lost
in contempt for the man I blamed for everything.
There was the time I was in love and he met my
boyfriend. Now he forgets to go to the bathroom

or where he is but he still remembers Michael
and asks about him. I help him walk slowly
outdoors to step outside the prison cell that is
the tiny apartment with no windows in which
I grew up abused by both of them. He barely
understands. His fate has been torture. I know
that I cannot be his savior. I used to pray for
him to die but here he is slowly fading. In his
eyes I see that he learned to love me and wishes
he could take it all back. He is unable to recall
those drunken nights and hateful words. I should

do the same. I left a long time ago but he still
remains haunted by the little boy who wanted
to belong. Like him, I want to forget that we
made mistakes and caused so much pain. I need
for both of us to remember how he taught me
how to ride a bike and how to swim and told
me, better late than never, that he loved me and
was proud of all I had done. I have to help him
settle into his favorite chair and let him know that
I forgive him. There is a place somewhere where
he will call me *hijo* and I will know him as my dad.

SAVIOR

FOR PIRI THOMAS

My vulnerability in front of an audience,
it provides connection. Electrical charge.
Approachable touch. Welcome embrace.
Deceit in fruition.

I stand upon this stage
a narcissistic prophet. Illuminating lights
providing halo effects.
Your Christ on a cross
until declaring myself gay.

There is no need to excuse
yourself from judgment.
I have learned to live within this box.
Yield assumptions of weakness with sassy comments.
Speak. A factory line homosexual creation
for American consumption.
Of course, I love Madonna and Broadway musicals.
Of course, I can fake the lisp of stereotypes.

But I am also more than Puerto Rican
heat and Ecuadorian mountains
baptized in Santero myths;
the causes you expect me to fight for;
expressing the tragedies of others, their struggles.
My heart is a casket
carrying the dead body of my boyhood soul
and the solitude of words never uttered.

My eyes are as dark as the rooms
in which children are abused.
Bright as the power of revelation.

Alive as the night sky.
I read from pages; avoid contact.
Girls and boys like us learn not to stare.

Live in my skin
if this fever is not too much to bear—
full of desire and passion.
The awkwardness of non-virgin children
reflecting abused adults in the mirror.

Our trust is a cold windy road
with no one around to guide us home,
lurking in shadows
much like animals you know are
there but cannot see.

I am capable of finding happiness.
Refusing to become all those
things I was left behind to be.
I am possible to love
because I have been hurt.
Safely emerging from so many hands,
secret hiding places intact.
Remembering only laughter.
Learning to talk to express pain
and pleasure and peace.

Silence cannot start conversations.
Poems are museums containing art.
They must be shared with others,
written by candlelight but read loudly,
holding nothing back.
Perhaps even saying too much
but never enough.

Yeah, I have warmed many beds.
Given freely of myself.
Joked to my own disadvantage
but my rest belongs to me.
I will sleep comfortably only with
the right one—not dictator, or tyrant,
or hypocrite—he who shares these dreams.

I am born anew at each A.M.
in the arms of my father figure.
Down these mean streets
I too have learned to survive.

THE WAY WE ARE
(OR PERHAPS JUST THE WAY THAT I AM)

There are no lullabies
for damaged children
used as sex slaves right out of cribs
Never a chance
to be wholesome

Self-destructively standing
on the edge of rooftops
to be swallowed up by the world below
No religion
available to heal our souls

You watch us lusting
drunk off intercourse
desiring affection from strangers
revisting torment

We give ourselves freely
disappoint when we don't
because we want what others can have—
to be more than broken toys

Our hearts—
love stories written with pencils
for simple erasure
until the next one comes along

We are house-trained animals
fodder for human friendship
until they settle and we are boring
tragic in our needs
fading unnoticed into the background

We are demons disguised as poets
falsely expressing concern for politics and social justice
infiltrating the respectable ranks of true artists

We are threatening in our free-spiritedness
comfortable in unknown beds
willing to fulfill fantasies
easily and too readily

We are temptation
darkness and decadance
covered by thick skin
daring and desirable
toned from all the running (away)
promising the casualness of laughter
sweet goodbyes in the morning
smiles on the subway ride home
and damned if we want anything more

We survive independently
express creatively
rock stars with devoted fans
loving the audacity we learned much too young

We are filled with loneliness
praying for someone to love us
to find that lost innocence
wanting our fathers
to save us
from monsters

STEPHEN ZERANCE

This is a Phase

MOSQUITO

Swatted four today on the wall as they danced
to waste. They know breathing.

They sense a warm body at night
from the leaves and shrubs they hide in.

The female travels to saw her mouth across skin,
to collect flesh to grow pregnant, cause

the bite on the skin, the infection, rather.
Once I was eight and fell into a nest,

wandered off the trail away from my sister,
touched the larvae hidden under ivy. All

up my arms, eruptions running through
the Blue Ridge Mountains.

And what of the males?

All they do is swarm at dusk, fuck, live
a week mostly concerned with nectar.

If given a choice, even in a lab, between
blood or sugar, they will always choose sugar.

VIRGIN

I am afraid to go into my room. She
is there after school, tidying, folding
my shirts—room spotless. She
asks *Why do you want to get sick?*
Why do you want filth in your mouth?
I'm a virgin and believe AIDS
hides inside the spinal cord. If
I have sex with a man, one day
it will release, a sort of magic. She
leaves an internet printout under
my pillow, a story of recovery
from a college boy. *This is normal.*
This is a phase.

When we fuck, I think too much
of the fire beneath sheets she
planted—the dirt on my palms
I can't scour, that constant rise
of skin when you pass through me
faster than the wild flowers
flying by down the long stretch
of highway—all Black-eyed
Susans, periwinkles, perfume.

STEPHEN ZERANCE

KOMODO DRAGON

With razor saliva, this giant needs just one bite.
Bacteria finish you off in one clot. Doesn't matter

how fast you get away, they smell for miles. Imagine
their discoverers, how remote the islands, beaches, water,

then falling asleep—in the morning, all that's left
is a bloody shoe, pair of glasses, and a few survivors'

bad stories. *Here be dragons*, first explorers scrawled
on maps. Milton said, *solitude is sometimes best society*.

How wrong with these cannibals, who rule with no
competition. In ancient times, dragons shared

land with a dwarf race of people with grapefruit-sized
heads. Skeletons of each were found in caves.

Who hunted whom? In island rule, if you want
something, wait for it. Swallow it whole—the hide,

hooves, the tourist. Isolate and grow large.
If devoured, emerge as skeleton, bone dressed

in the finest suit—a coat out of the ribs, the sternum
playing a tie, the clavicle, a collar.

TICK

Pick one of the doors in the hallway.
Open it, lock yourself inside. Exhaust
all items in the room. Cram them

in your heart's lock box. Eat every
crumb. Put your feet on the furniture.
Hitch a ride. Pass for a deadbeat.

May. My mother warns they emerge.
Afternoons, my sister and I survey
our hair, legs, skin we cannot see.

When she strikes the match,
I'm on the mud room floor—shorts
rolled, with a black tab—too deep

to pull out behind my knee. The tick
rushes, eight legs disappear into skin.
I prepare for bull's-eye mornings,

wear pants all summer long. Those
checks where I combed over my body
in witch hunt, undressing

to spot the mark of parasite, where
if finding nothing meant it must
be buried inside, that health

is a sleeve,
an outfit placed on daily
panic, nudity—a great deal of it.

RITUAL

Slice me nice
where you work
down my back,
pierce my spine
into a hawk
with thirteen bronze
pins so I may
think of you.

I walk around
the neighborhood
three times
to find my lover
gone. A street
with each car's
windows bashed out
passenger side
offers me the city
I desire, the rooms
of my mind.

I come home
to find a window
open, broken into.
A man had walked
into my life,
had looked around,
had stolen nothing—

but painted
my body turquoise,
double-headed serpent

STEPHEN ZERANCE

in the throws of July,
to dart into mouths
to lap the precious water,
to dance bewitched,
dancing mad.

IN SECONDS

Second story on the news: second
story rapist strikes through fire escapes—

The lesbian couple above me swears
they hear footsteps on metal at night,

tapes a police sketch of the man
outside their window, installs bars

after a knife-point victim was held
a street away. Around the world

people report visitations of a shadow
man of smokeless flame

in corners of the room observing
consciousness. I stopped dead to check

my pulse on the sidewalk today,
near an alley where a homeless

man now stands silent, shirtless
leaning against a staff for hours.

I understand nothing at night,
dream of peeling my feet ankle

to toe, waiting days on the bed
until they freshen and awake heart

in mouth to think how we prowl—
live only blocks removed, yet we deny

comfort—the inner malady
being forced out.

MARSYAS

The radiator's hiss catcalls me
      out the door, ribcage and pale
limbs in a tank top three sizes

too large. I'm angel of my corner bar,
with no problem going alone, lonely
      as I am, Stranger. I drink

until one eye is bigger than the other,
   until I talk close to you, blue and
      glass eyed. Tear me away

      from myself, through the open veins
of the city—golden and skinned alive
   into dawn, through doorway to you.

   I am knife thin, Stranger, thinner than reed
      slit between the teeth. Thinner
than pitted string on the lyre. Do

as you please tonight. I do not like
      to be touched on my back, that one
wound that rings as the music—

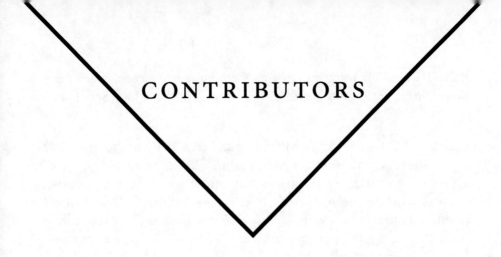

CONTRIBUTORS

DERRICK AUSTIN is an MFA candidate at the University of Michigan. His work has appeared or is forthcoming in *Unsplendid, Tampa Review Online, Knockout, Crab Orchard Review,* and other journals. He is assistant poetry editor at *The Nervous Breakdown.*

DAVID BERGMAN is the author of four books of poetry, the latest of which is *Fortunate Light.* He won the George Elliston prize for his first book *Cracking the Code.* He edited John Ashbery's collected art writing *Reported Sightings* and *Gay American Autobiography.* He teaches at Towson University and lives in Baltimore.

JOE ELDRIDGE earned his MFA in Poetry at Columbia College Chicago where he is currently an adjunct professor teaching in the poetry, literature & speech departments. He has published poems in *The Gay & Lesbian Review, Court Green, Velvet Mafia, Up the Staircase, St. Sebastian's Review, Zygote in My Coffee, Fickle Muses, Columbia Poetry Review, Moonshot, The Apocalypse, Clementine, Vine Leaves, The Literary Underground, OVS,* and *Turbulence.* Eldridge is also a flight attendant for a major airline with 28 years seniority and works on weekends as a purser mainly to Europe and Asia. A black belt in Seido karate, Sempai Joe, who trains at Thousand Waves Martial Arts and Self-Defense Center NFP, won the gold medal in men's black belt sparring at Gay Games VII aka the Chicago Gaymes.

CONTRIBUTORS

ROBERT HEALD, a native of Atlanta, Georgia, is an undergraduate student at Colorado College. He wishes his bio was longer, but this is his first publication.

GARY LUNDY taught English literature and creative writing for twenty years at The University of Montana Western, in Dillon, Montana. His poetry has appeared in a variety of magazines and journals, most recently *Askew, My Favorite Bullet* (online), *Cedilla, Indefinite Space, Citizens for Decent Literature* (online), *Prairie Winds*, and *The Prague Revue* (online). He is the author of three chapbooks, *this making i tore the sight from* (Sweetbrier Press, 1996), *lavish is saying nothing like again* (Blue Malady Press, 1997), and *to each other water cool and pure* (Blue Malady Press, 2003). His new chapbook, *when voices detach themselves*, will be published in the fall of 2013 by is a rose press. Gary now lives in Missoula, Montana. [facebook.com/gary.lundy.14]

JEFF OAKS' newest chapbook, *Mistakes with Strangers*, will be published by Seven Kitchens Press in 2013. His poem "Saint Wrench" was selected for *Best New Poets 2012* by Matthew Dickman. A recipient of three Pennsylvania Council of the Arts fellowships, his poems have appeared most recently in *Prairie Schooner, Rhino, Barrow Street*, and *Field*. His essays have appeared most recently in *At Length, Creative Nonfiction*, and *My Diva: 65 Gay Men on the Women Who Inspire Them*. He teaches writing at the University of Pittsburgh.

CHRISTOPHER PHELPS studied science and philosophy, disciplines that continue to fascinate, inform, and subvert his poetics. His poems appear in magazines including *Boston Review, Field, The Kenyon Review, The New Republic, Washington Square*, and in the anthology *Collective Brightness: LGBTIQ Poets on Faith, Religion and Spirituality*. [christopher-phelps.com.]

STEVEN RIEL is the author of three chapbooks of poetry: *How to Dream, The Spirit Can Crest*, and most recently, *Postcard from P-town*, which was selected as runner-up for the inaugural Robin Becker Chapbook Prize and published in 2009 by Seven Kitchens Press. He was named the 2005 Robert Fraser Distinguished Visiting Poet at Bucks County (PA) Community College. His poems have appeared in several anthologies and in numerous periodicals, including *The Minnesota Review*, *International Poetry Review*, and *Evening Street Review*. He served as poetry editor of *RFD* between 1987 and 1995. He received an MFA in 2008 from New England College. The Massachusetts Cultural Council awarded him a grant in 1992. One of his poems was selected by Denise Levertov as runner-up for the Grolier Poetry Peace Prize in 1987.

JACKSON SABBAGH is from Salem, Massachusetts. He is a 20-year-old junior, studying creative writing at Sarah Lawrence College, and is currently on his year abroad at Oxford University, England. He's a gay male, and has been probably for life, ever since his 6-year-old adventures with his best friend in his bathroom. When it came time for college (he had come out the summer before) he began his forays into both worlds, poetry and the gay landscape. Poetry immediately became a healthy arena for intellectual performance (the workshop space), and he simultaneously began performing in the gay circles of his college as "slutty," "open," "naïve," and other adjectives which make him giddy to be described as. He hopes only to live up to them.

ROBERT WHITEHEAD received his MFA from Washington University in St. Louis. He currently lives in Brooklyn.

EMANUEL XAVIER, an Equality Forum LGBT History Month Icon, is an award-winning NYC based poet best known for his appearances on *Russell Simmons presents Def Poetry on HBO*. *Pier Queen* was officially published in 2012 along with a revised edition of his poetry collection, *Americano: Growing up Gay and Latino in the USA*. He is also author of *If Jesus Were Gay & other poems* and the novel *Christ Like* and editor of *Mariposas: A Modern Anthology of Queer Latino Poetry* and *Me No Habla With Acento: Contemporary Latino Poetry*. His work also appears in the books *For Colored Boys Who Have Considered Suicide When the Rainbow is Still Not Enough* and *Born This Way: Real Stories of Growing Up Gay* based on the popular blog. His new poetry collection is *Nefarious* (Rebel Satori Press, 2013). [emanuelxavier.com]

STEPHEN ZERANCE is a recent MFA graduate of American University. He has previously appeared or is forthcoming in journals such as *Prairie Schooner, Bloom, Knockout, Chelsea Station, Gay and Lesbian Review Worldwide*, and *MiPOesias*. His work has also been featured on websites such as Lambda

Literary and Split This Rock. He resides in Baltimore, Maryland.

CODY HENSLEE [Cover Photographer] also provided the cover image for the third issue of *Assaracus*, and thus becomes the first two-time *Assaracus* cover artist. He is currently working with social assumptions concerning groups of people rather than focusing solely on the individual. The series "Heels-Boys-Grimes," from which the cover photograph was selected, combines his interest in the elements of pop, sexual orientation, and social assumptions. This series plays with the viewer's ability to place assumptions within the content of the image, and by doing so, the content of the image shifts from viewer to viewer. As an artist, Cody finds comfort in knowing that his art exists beyond his control and within a realm that allows it to grow and transform. This photograph features **PADEN HAYNES**.

SETH PENNINGTON [Associate Editor of Sibling Rivalry Press] lives in Alexander, Arkansas, with his husband, Bryan. [sethpennington.wordpress.com]

BRYAN BORLAND [Editor of *Assaracus*] lives in Alexander, Arkansas, with his husband, Seth. [bryanborland.com]

SUBMIT TO *ASSARACUS*

We encourage submissions to *Assaracus* by gay male poets of any age, regardless of background, education, or level of publication experience. Submissions are accepted during the months of January, May, and September. For more information, visit us online. [siblingrivalrypress.com]

SUBSCRIBE TO *ASSARACUS*

Visit our website to subscribe to *Assaracus*. Your subscription buys you four book-length (120+ pages), perfect-bound issues of our grand stage for gay contemporary poetry. Our standard subscription prices are $50.00 for one year/United States; $80.00 for one year/international. Inspired by the long-running journal *Sinister Wisdom*, we are also proud to offer a special hardship subscription price of $20.00, which includes four issues of *Assaracus* shipped anywhere in the world. We ask that you pay full price should you have the ability to do so, but one's degree of good fortune should never impede access to poetry. Likewise, we will provide free copies of *Assaracus* to LGBTIQ support groups, mental health facilities, and correctional facilities by request. To request a free copy or subscription, please email us. We also offer the option of voluntary "sustaining subscriptions" for various dollar amounts should you wish to financially contribute to the longevity of *Assaracus*. Such support will also help us to continue offering discounted and free issues of the journal to those who might benefit. [siblingrivalrypress.com]

NEW FROM SIBLING RIVALRY PRESS

New books from *Assaracus* contributors Christopher Gaskins (*Boys have been...*) and Robert Siek (*Purpose and Devil Piss*).